The Bumpy Journey

*How to Survive and Thrive in your Baby's
First Three Years*

Cheryl Jerabek

D1315392

Acknowledgments

I would like to recognize, acknowledge and applaud all the people around the world that helped make this book and this mission possible. I cannot name you all individually, but you know who you are. I' am honored to serve with you on this noble mission of educating the world and helping each person becoming a better person today than he was yesterday.

I would like to specifically highlight and mention those individuals who were directly instrumental in the writing and publishing of this book: Heather Hilliard, Yola Angeline Alonzo, Cheryl Green, Minerva Buenaluz, Shilpy Law and all the wonderful people of Digital Print House for their support and assistance toward creating this material.

Table of Contents

Introduction

Are you really ready for motherhood? Mothers are often caught off guard and fathers thrown for a loop when the baby bump becomes a real, live bundle. While babies are miracles with their tiny toes and little pink cheeks, they are also a handful. But there are things that can help prepare you for motherhood and this book is for the soon-to-be and new moms.

For instance, by the time your little one is potty trained, you will have changed 7,000 to 9,000 diapers. While you probably know how to change a disposable diaper, some babies have skin so sensitive that they cannot tolerate disposables. You may not have known that the disposable diapers used in America alone account for 7.9 billion pounds of garbage per year. It is estimated that up to one-third of mothers in the United States are now turning to cloth diapers. If you decide to use cloth (or your baby makes that decision for you), this book will not only give you instructions, you'll learn how to fold them as well.

There are tons of questions you will have as you begin your journey into motherhood. Just when you think you have it all together, you will be overwhelmed with the realization that there is so much more to learn. There always is. That's the essence of motherhood — it's a mix of winging it and learning as you go.

That's how this book helps you. It is the instruction manual that you wished had been handed to you with your baby. Not only will you learn tips on how to take care of your baby, you'll learn some behind-the-scene information, too. You'll learn *why* a baby's brain is programed to turn when her cheek is touched, *what* hormone causes your milk to draw when you hear your little boy cry. You'll also learn things about *when* your little one's brain is stimulated when she begins to engage in different types of play and *how* play stimulates cognitive development.

As if it's not enough for this book to include what you need to know in order to raise your baby for the first two years of her life, there's more. We talk about you. If you don't take care of yourself, you won't be able to properly take care of your little one. And, what about your relationship with your partner? You need to take time to nurture your partnership so that you don't lose yourselves in everything for the baby.

We also approach the hard fact that your stress spills over to your baby. It physically stunts his brain development or she may not be fully restful. Motherhood is stressful but with knowledge and support, you can find ways to revive so you can thrive. You'll be a much better mother when you take time for yourself, too, and make things easier than need completed on a regular basis.

Dive into this book and use it as a resource to find out about things like support groups for nursing mothers, how to deal with intrusive in-laws and so much more. You'll get inside information on subjects like your baby's growth and development, what is taking place within her eating habits at various stages, how his social skills are developing and you'll learn different methods of age appropriate discipline.

There's never been such a well-rounded book to help you walk through the pathways you'll encounter as you embark on the wonderful journey that awaits you. This book will be a shed light on ways to prepare and can help guide you in the stressful times that are inevitably part of raising children. You will also learn how to take a deep breath and see the miracles unraveling before you with a fresh, new perspective on it all.

Though the first two years of your baby's life may seem to last forever, blink and they are gone. Enjoy the time for yourself and for her. A prepared mother is a good mother. This book is with you every step of the way to help lead you. Motherhood is about progress, not perfection. Unreal expectations on yourself and your little one can spoil the view. It's a beautiful journey. Don't wait another day. Let's get started!

Laying a Firm Foundation

"Babies change things, open doors you thought were shut, close others.
Make you into something you've never been."

- Dorothy Allison

So you're going to have a new addition to the family. Congratulations! Your family will now be picture perfect. Well... almost. Although there will be some imperfections in the family portrait as your family first starts to grow, with some insight and inspiration you can certainly make it into a masterpiece.

Let's start at the beginning. One thing to anticipate as you prepare for your new arrival is that diapers won't be the only thing that will be changing. You're whole life is about to change, including your relationship. It might get better. It might get worse. But, you can prepare for some "typical" situations when your little one joins the family.

The notion that having a baby can take a toll on a relationship may be hard to understand since it's usually out of love that a baby is coming into your home. You may not be able to imagine how it could possibly do anything other than to enhance the relationship between the two of you. Infatuation with the very thought of motherhood is quite natural and very healthy, to an extent. But eventually, infatuation gives way to reality.

The good news is that the more you know, the more you can do to ensure that your family grows together rather than apart. Generally it takes hard work from both sides and the same holds true for healthy marriages staying healthy. You must build a firm foundation so that your relationship will stand, even when things get rocky. Let's take a look behind the scenes at what that really entails.

Matters of the Mind versus Matters of the Heart

There are a number of trials and tribulations that your new baby will bring. It's not her fault. She's just a baby doing what babies do. Infants eat, sleep, poop and cry. They sometimes stay up all night, scream for hours and get very demanding.

Don't worry. The rough times will make the good times that much better. Chances are pretty good that you'll survive your child's early years. But… will your relationship? That's the million dollar question.

There are about 18 inches between our head and our heart. Sometimes, it's as if they are billions of miles apart. Many of us, especially new mothers but truly all new parents, are guilty of making decisions using just our heart or, in rarer instance, just our brain. Relying on either one can get you into trouble where your relationship is concerned.

Brain

In the New York Times best-seller book "Brain Rules for Baby," the author, Dr. John Medina, explains how our brain really works. A developmental molecular biologist, Medina has spent a good portion of his career researching and consulting mental health, namely in the biotech and pharmaceutical fields. He has focused on early childhood development and on parent relationships as well.

In the book, Medina addresses some of the relationship issues that new parents are likely to encounter. He teaches what is actually going on inside the brain and how it all falls together in reality. While the heart oftentimes is ruled by emotions and feelings, his viewpoint is shared from the scientific angle (which certainly helps to provide soon-to-be or new parents a balance).

When your brain runs the show, you likely won't have a spoiled baby or a partner that feels neglected. In fact, the opposite is likely to happen. You may be extremely rigid with yourself, your child and your spouse. In short, if you are too "brain oriented" in your child rearing, you most likely will rule with an iron fist and run your household and your relationships like an Army Sergeant.

Heart

The love you will have for your newborn baby is overwhelming. It is engulfing, all encompassing. There is nothing like the bond between mother and child. The fact that your  infant is totally dependent upon you also adds more emotion to the equation.

You might not know it, but your heart and your emotions are actually run by your brain. In fact, the very feelings that set the stage in your relationship that brought you to be parents was stimulated by your brain and hormones. They also are the "feel good" hormones released during childbirth and during cuddling of your infant. When you share these feelings with your baby, you need to make sure to have time and feelings for your partner, too.

It takes a balance of heart and brain for a relationship to flourish. Sometimes it's best to do the right thing (a brain decision), regardless of how you emotionally feel about it (your heart decision). Examples of conflicting situations for new parents where your "brain" should win include letting your baby "cry it out" or sticking to a schedule you know is best. Other times, your heart will guide you.

It is in having the wisdom to know when it's best to do one or the other or both that will ultimately make for a successful relationship, and you learn these as you go (and from the chapters in this book). When you work together to raise your baby, the bumps in the road are easier to handle together.

Baby-Bourne Bumps in the Road

There is no doubt that there are difficulties that new parents face. Here are some of the issues that are the most common and how you can deal with them together and what you need to do for yourself.

Sleep loss

Seven days without sleep makes anyone weak... and that's an understatement. Although babies sleep anywhere from 16 to 17 hours a day, that certainly doesn't going to mean that parents will. It is estimated that 70% of newborn parents are seriously sleep deprived. Needless to say, that awakens the beast in most of us.

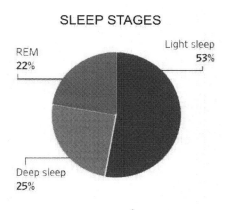

SLEEP STAGES

REM 22%

Light sleep 53%

Deep sleep 25%

Sleep is necessary to repair, renew, rejuvenate and grow. According to the American Sleep Association, there are five stages of sleep and it's important for parents to be well-rested as they help their little one grow.

Sleep is science-oriented. Nerve cells (neurons) produce a chemical called neurotransmitters that send out signals to various part of the brain. They shut down areas where thinking and learning occur when it's time to get some sleep while the sleep areas of the brain become more active. Once sleep is achieved, the signals decrease in the sleep centered brain areas and increase in the areas where thinking, learning, communicating and other such functions originate. That explains why we don't function very well when we are sleepy and over-tired since all the energy is being used elsewhere.

Is any sleep good sleep? Of course, it's better to get some sleep rather than none at all. As a new mother, you'll no doubt take what you can get. But beware that you will be short-changed if fragmented sleep is all you get (as it probably will be, for the first few months at least).

While disrupted sleep cannot really be avoided with a little one's needs calling all the shots, here are some symptoms that may occur that you and your partner should know if you are sleep-deprived.

- Depression

- Foggy thoughts

- Grogginess

- Irritability

- Chronic tiredness

- Inability to fight off illness

- Excessive worry

- Irritability

The relationship of each family member (even the baby) is compared to spokes on a wheel. When any of the spokes are not in alignment, the wheel won't function correctly. You can only imagine the scenario when mom's spoke is misaligned. It's important to do all that you can to remain on a good sleep cycle.

Here are some suggestions for improving your sleep:

- Ask your spouse to take over a shift for you so that you can get some GOOD rest. If he is off on the week-ends, you might consider having him take on a Saturday night for you. While it might seem selfish to ask, it's important to realize that it's not. It will give you a much needed break and you can come back as a better spoke.

- Soak in a hot bath of lavender essential oil mixed with a coconut, jojoba or olive oil and soothe your cares away.

- Take some time for you and your spouse. While this doesn't necessarily get you more sleep, it is good for your relationship. Take advantage of family members who offer to watch the little one or find a trustworthy babysitter. By enhancing your relationship, you are more likely to rest easier when you do sleep.

- Invest in a CD of relaxing music or better yet, noises from nature like waterfalls and ocean waves. Play it as you are trying to fall asleep.

- Download or purchase a fiction book that has nothing to do with babies and read it before bed.

Study up on ways to encourage your baby to sleep better and longer. When your baby sleeps, it's a good idea for you to sleep, too. While it's tempting to get housework done during the time she is snoozing, it's better in the long run to catch up on your own zzzz's.

Social isolation

Being a new mom can often leave you "home alone" as far as interaction with other adults. Getting your little one out may not be practical or even wise in many cases, so you most likely will find yourself more isolated than you are used to being. This can be stressful and it's completely normal to have such feelings. Humans are social beings. We are set up to be that way for a reason so when you are not interacting, you are supposed to feel that something's not right.

According to a study performed by the UK-based company Nurofen for Children and Babies, when they talked to 2,000 new moms, 55 percent admitted they missed their pre-baby social life and 51 percent missed their pre-baby body. Loneliness can open the door for more serious issues like depression or even stress-aggravated illnesses such as diseases like diabetes and heart conditions. But here are some suggestions on how to constructively deal with the situation.

Accept it. Accepting the things you cannot change is part of coming to peace with any given situation. Being a new mother is certainly a situation that warrants peace. While the joys of motherhood far outweigh the drawbacks, it's normal to find it difficult to let go of your pre-baby lifestyle sometimes. There will be some things that simply won't fit into your life now. That's when it's time to just let it go and face the fact that being a new mom has both priceless moments and price-tags, too.

Go with it. You may not get to do all the things you used to do now that you have a little one, but the good news is that it brings you to do some things you weren't eligible to do before. You can enroll in new mother clubs and groups. You can start checking into play groups you will want to join once your little one begins to interact with others. Get together with friends and family members who have babies and keep your eyes peeled for new mothers you can get to know.

Substitute it. If you aren't able to socialize because you are opting not to take your baby out, bring some interaction into the house. Social media sites, like Facebook and Instagram, offer a great alternative for face-to-face communication. You can also email friends, Skype, create Vines for other new mothers, make YouTube videos about your adventure sin motherhood and many other things that are available thanks to new technology.

Unequal workload

As a new mother, you will probably notice that you are doing more than ever, which may entail that you are also doing more than your spouse or partner. Welcome to motherhood! But, although this is typical to an extent, it should never be terrible unbalanced.

You are not the only one who should be doing more. You are both parents now so you should both be doing more. Sure, there will be things that only you can do, like nursing, but there is a long list of things that he CAN do to help (like bottle feeding at night if you prepare bottles by pumping breast milk during the day or show your partner how to make a bottle with the formula).

There are many people with suggestions on balancing the parental workload. Dr. Medina suggests making a list of what chores each parent completes daily. If it is off-balance, adjust the list. Renegotiate the things that need done. Your husband may need a little prompting to create the list or you can even do it for him but it is imperative to go over it together and to do so in love, not anger.

Together, the two of you have a child. Now, the two of you have a list in writing and can work together on sharing house roles and parenting roles. Having a less-stressed mom are well worth the efforts.

Depression

Depression hurts more than just the one who is depressed. It hurts the entire family. If you are depressed, it will flow over to into your entire household and even to your other relationships.

It's very normal to experience depression after the birth of your baby. According to research published on ScienceDaily.com, up to 70 percent of new mothers feel sad or depressed during the first week of their baby's life. Your hormones are high from the birth. The changes in estrogen alone dramatically fluctuate during the first week when it's usually lowest on the fifth day. This changes in hormones wreaks havoc on your body physically and emotionally as well.

There are other reasons for depression. There are new responsibilities, you are sleep deprived and everything is new. You likely have new fears, too.

Most recover very quickly and without the need for treatment. As you adjust to the new home environment and the shift in roles, your anxiety decreases (which contributes to depression). You gradually become the happy mom, less anxious and less depressed as you grow more confident as a parent.

Here are some things that might help lift your spirits:

- Take a little "me time" out. Soak in a bubble bath, read in a good book or go have your nails done while your partner spends quality time with the baby.

- Talk to someone. Whether it's a trusted friend or even a counselor, expressing how you feel should help you feel better and learn that you aren't the first one that's experienced these feelings.

- Get physical. Exercise helps to lift depression. Have someone watch the baby while you go to the gym or walk around the block. You'll stimulate your body's natural defenses to depression. If you can't get a sitter, put the baby in the stroller for some nap time miles while you get fresh air, too.

If you are not finding your depression lessening, talk to your physician. Postpartum depression is a very real and very serious medical condition and there are solutions.

Relationships beyond the Bump

Sex

Sure enough, it turns out that saving the date might just save your marriage, too. Most couples report a dramatic decline in their sexual relations after the birth of a baby. If you're not  careful, you may find that days, weeks, or even months pass by without having sex. You may be too busy to notice but you partner may be all too aware that time is passing.

There are a number of reasons that sex may fall by the wayside. One is that you become quite busy with your new little one. Another is that you may not feel the desires you once did, mostly attributed to physical and mental exhaustion.

There are a myriad of reasons you may not be having sex, but there are every bit the amount of reasons why you should. Making love brings couples to grow closer, in all aspects. It is an emotional fulfillment and also revives your body physically.

If your love life is lacking, here are some suggestions:

- Watch a romantic movie together.

- Get a sitter and go out on a date.

- Remember the things that originally attracted you to each other.

- Get some sleep so your body isn't so tired.

- Flirt with your partner.

- Read a steamy novel.

- Take a hot bubble bath with soft music playing.

- Share a candlelit dinner together

- Circle a day on the calendar and enjoy!

The more you do to set the mood, the more romantic will feel. Think back to how things used to be prior to baby and bring some of the former things into your relationship now. Focus on fun and fulfillment, not on obligation and you'll be much better for it.

Money

Money isn't usually a problem in a marriage, but the lack of it sure is. Having a baby fills your heart and drains your wallet. Estimates show that raising a child in 2016 costs approximately $245,340.00 for the average family according to the Wall Street Journal.

There is no getting around it — having a baby will deplete your bank account. There are all sorts of expenses: diapers, medical bills, insurance, clothes, a sitter if you are going back to work... the list just keeps mounting. Once college arrives, you know there won't be any relief there.

What you can do to prepare, though, is twofold. Create and adhere to a budget. You will both give up some special treats (perhaps there's limited shoe shopping and nights out to eat). You can save on cable services, look for deals on cellular plans or even look for coupons for things that are non-perishable to get better deals on timing or quantity. A good look at your budget should give way to finding some creative cuts that can be implemented.

Communication channels being open between the two of you also keeps things flowing. When you aren't discussing money matters, chances are high that you are internalizing stressful feelings and are becoming resentful of money concerns. Remember that talking cents makes sense.

Parenting Styles Divergence

He is all for letting baby cry herself to sleep. He fully believes she will learn to self-soothe and life will then be better for all. You, on the other hand, are mortified at the very thought of letting her cry, at all… for anything. You are a firm believer that it is your job to make sure her world is a stress-free, peaceful environment which will encourage her to flourish.

It's not a bad idea to get some understanding on parenting styles before you become pregnant or at least before the baby is born. But, if you are finding that the two of you don't see eye-to-eye, join the crowd. Many new parents discover they have completely different parenting concepts.

Communication is key. Perhaps all you understand from talking about parenting concepts is that he thinks the baby should cry it out and you have no clue why. But, once he lets you know that she is likely to find solace and be able to problem-solve later in life, the idea might make much more sense to you.

Compromise is important, too. Agree to disagree and go a step beyond to do the best you can to blend your ideals into a workable plan. The two of you will need to work together for many years to come. Do your best to do what's best… for yourselves and baby, too.

In-laws

Consider yourself forewarned. Mother-in-laws (and even father-in-laws) have been known to interfere with not only marriages, but child rearing, too. Have you ever seen the movie, "Monster in Law"? Sadly, the movie rings true to many parents, especially new parents.

According to an article written in July of 2009, entitled "Five Biggest Mistakes of Mothers-in-Law" published by Newsweek Magazine, the situation can be grave for a marriage. The article also included information about an Italian study conducted by the National Statistics Institute concluded that for each hundred yards away that a couple lived from their in-laws, it increased their chances of a successful marriage.

It may start out as friendly advice, but it's not unusual for grandparents to get more and more vocal and demanding in addition to in-laws. While it doesn't make it right, you have to stop and consider that the baby does have their genes. That doesn't give them the right to raise the child or to interfere, but, it does explain a little bit of the reason behind it.

One thing that may help you cope with such unsolicited advice is to see the flip-side. It's nice to know that others beside the two parents are wild about the baby. The bond between a grandparent and their grandchild is a mighty one, which should warm your heart and will hopefully raise your tolerance a notch as well.

Always remember that you as the parent have the final say. Although suggestions and advice may get on your last nerve, grandparents hold no power that you do not give them. You might consider the things they say; sometimes grandparents are wise. But, sometimes they are simply intrusive. It is up to you and your spouse to determine the amount of recommendation versus toleration needed in the relationship.

Other Relationship Matters

By now you may be feeling a bit overwhelmed with all the things that you have to accomplish when you welcome your little one home. Babies are rough on a marriage. Just marriage is tough on a marriage so adding one more person to the equation complicates the relationship even further. But, your baby is a miracle of the love you share. While, having a baby is not all roses, with lots of love and some diligent effort, your relationship will bloom and become stronger than ever. But this time of awaiting the baby's arrival is also a time when your relationship with yourself if changing, too.

Pregnancy is a time of preparation. As your baby develops, so are new aspects of you. You are being molded into a parent. Every morning when you wake up, every single change is priming you for becoming a mom. It is perfectly natural to have emotions of a roller coaster that you are so ready to welcome the child into your life, and then you realize you may have forgotten some preparation steps - such as the nursery and... it's bare. Your emotions have gone from pleasure to panic in less than a minute. That will be a way of life for the next eighteen or so years.

It's very natural to go from one extreme to the other. The reality is that this feeling of extremes is part of your preparation for parenthood. You will feel like the best mother and the worst, all in one day. The fact of the matter is that you will most likely be neither the best mom nor the worst. But as long as you are the best mother that you can be, you'll have this "parenting thing" down.

Worry is wasted energy. Doing something about your fears or the gaps you haven't addressed is much more constructive. So, let's take an inventory of what you will need before your baby arrives.

As with all things when it comes to motherhood, it is progress not perfection that counts. If you don't have something crossed off the list by the time your baby is born, it's not the end of the world. Many babies have survived without the perfect going-home outfit and some have slept in makeshift bassinets. It's much more important to bring your baby into a safe, calm and peaceful environment than it is to work yourself up about everything being just right. So relax and give yourself a break; get what you can, as you can.

Getting Your Rear in Gear

It's common for expectant mothers to have a spontaneous need to clean and organize the baby's things in the very last stages of their pregnancy. This is affectionately termed nesting. If the notion strikes you, by all means nest. But, do be wise. Many women have gone into labor a little ahead of time due to over-scrubbing the floor or rearranging furniture they shouldn't be lifting.

Exercise is important, even when you are nearing the end of your pregnancy. It helps to reduce anxiety and stress which definitely can be present during this time. And remember that the more fit you are, your chances are better for a smoother delivery. That's reason enough to exercise right there!

Both nesting and exercise certainly should be done within reason and at level that you are physically and mentally comfortable with. Nest safely!

Chapter Takeaways

1. You will need a lot of things for your baby but very few are so essential you can't do without them. Do not stress over baby items. Get what you can when you can.

2. It will take some work to keep up a great relationship with your spouse, but it will make you closer as well as help you raise your child in a strong, healthy home.

3. You may feel socially deprived with your new role as a parent but there are things you can do to remedy that.

4. Be sure that you don't stock up on too many newborn size clothes as your little one may just turn out to be a big one. They grow quickly, so having some larger sizes early on may be handy.

5. Nursing pillows make you and baby more comfortable during feeding time and baby slings are priceless because they allow you to get a few things done with baby in tow.

Bonus List: Top 25 Most Essential Baby Items

1. Car Seat

It's the law! But, even if a car seat wasn't legally mandatory, you'd want one anyway because they're safe and your number one job as a parent will be to keep your child out of harm's way.

Tragically, each year there are over 1.2 million people killed in car accidents worldwide. Injuries occurring on the road are the leading culprit of accidental child deaths in the United States. The good news is that by using a car seat correctly, the National Highway Traffic Safety Administration reviewed fatal car accident data and saw fatality risk is reduced by an estimated 71 percent. THAT's why you not only need, but want, a car seat.

You will be required to have a car seat when you bring your baby home. Most likely, you will be shown how to properly strap your newborn into the seat, but it's a good idea to know before you go all the same. The exact specifications of car seat requirements are set by state law so it's a good idea to check with your state online or in person to see what your state's standards are. Many police departments offer training on installing the car seat properly so you are ready before you go to the hospital. (It's also good to be on the safe side and ask what the hospital you are going to requires as well as hospitals vary as well.)

In the event that you can't afford a car seat or have your baby early and don't have one yet, some hospitals will work something out with you. Some let you buy one of theirs. Some hospitals may give you a discounted price and others give them at no charge to those who meet certain qualifications. There's never a good reason to not have a car seat.

2. Diapers and Wipers

One thing is for sure and for certain, you'll need diapers for your baby. And plenty of them! Most newborns go through 10-15 diapers per day.

When it comes to what kind of diaper to use, there are pros and cons to each. Choices include disposable and cloth. Pretty easy, right? Wrong. There are a myriad to choose from in both types. Let's take a look in this overview (more details are in the next chapter).

Disposables are the most popular pick. They are quick and convenient. But drawbacks on disposables are that they are expensive and can be harsh on your baby's sensitive skin (though there are special types for sensitive skin). You can catch sales and use coupons and incentives to help combat the expense, or buy in bulk at large "big box" stores. Disposables are also not eco-friendly. There are also organic brands and "green diapers" available in some locations, like Bamboo Nature and Earth's Best Tender Care. (Expect to pay more for organic, green ones though.)

Cloth diapers are another option. Some moms use them for economic or ecological reasons while others choose them because they are easier on their baby's sensitive skin. Cloth diapers must be washed (on the sterilize cycle), folded and the process is repeated over and over. You can use disposable diaper liners to help with the clean-up and can also opt for a diaper service (where available) that will come to your home, pick up the dirty diapers and deliver fresh sets all clean and folded. The downside to that is the service does have an additional expense so if you are using cloth diapers in order to save money, doing so might defeat the purpose.

In either disposables or cloth, you need to evaluate which brand is best for your family's needs. Although you can read reviews and ask other mothers for their opinions, trial and error will most likely be the only way to find out for sure. Babies are all built differently. While one diaper may fit one baby snug and securely, it may be too tight or loose for the next infant. If you have more than one child, you may see that the diaper you swore by for your first baby was a terrible choice for your second. Just keep "trying them on for size" and it will (eventually) all work out in the end.

As far as diaper wipes and creams are concerned, again, some mothers choose saving money and Mother Earth over convenience. Baby wash cloths for changing time can be purchased for next to nothing but they can be quite a mess, too. Disposable wipes are much more convenient but the cost of them can certainly add up; also, some babies' skin cannot tolerate them. There are still solutions for so many different issues, because you aren't the first parent to experience the issue! For example, if your baby has a reaction to wipes, you might try the hypo-allergenic ones. You can also find wipes in organic and eco-friendly versions, too.

3. Coming Home Outfit

This one is just for you! Your baby will not care how she is dressed to come home from the hospital unless you dress her in something that is really uncomfortable. But, if you're like most mothers, dolling your baby up for that memorable moment of welcoming her to her new home IS a big deal for you and a nicety you deserve. And, it does make for great pictures.

Traditionally, babies wore a formal or frilly outfit home from the hospital, but times are changing. A cute and comfy onesie or warm-up suit is a more popular choice these days. If you are set on a really fancy but uncomfortable outfit, you can always dress your baby in it long enough to snap some photos and then change her into something more appropriate. Hospitals have baby t-shirts or onesies so if you didn't get around to buying special duds, don't despair — and someone will surely visit you at the hospital and may bring you the perfect outfit, too. The fact that you are bringing your baby home is the main thing to be celebrated. The clothes are just icing on the cake.

4. Breast Pump

Even if you don't plan to leave your baby early in your home stay, you will want to have a breast pump just in case. Should an emergency arrive, you'll be set. A pump can also come in useful if your breasts become engorged or your milk supply is not adequate during a feeding. You can find one fairly inexpensive or opt for a hospital-grade one. Oftentimes, pumps are covered by medical insurance and some hospitals rent them out so you ask before your due date.

5. Bottles and Formula

Just as with a breast pump, even if you have no plans to bottle feed your baby, you will want to have a bottle or two on hand. You never know. Life with a baby can be very unpredictable and you don't want to be caught off guard. This is an overview, but more details are given in the "Feeding Frenzy" chapter.

It's a good idea to go with BPA-free bottles (which includes glass versions). You can find breast-mimicking nipples or opt for traditional ones. Babies are all different so you may need to experiment around before finding one that she likes. You can also choose to use bottles with liners which eliminates the need of sterilizing them.

There's another trick with bottle feeding that frustrates new parents until they figure it out (but usually are told about this point). Know that the hole in the nipples come in various sizes. That means a hungry child may eat for twenty minutes, but only sleep thirty and be hungry again because it can't suckle enough milk through the tiny hole in the nipple. Likewise, a slower eater may find a nipple hole too big and get air in her tummy, causing her to spit up more. This is a case of trying different ones and noting which your baby prefers.

As far as formula, there are powders and pre-mixed fluid options. In both of these categories, organic is becoming a very popular choice. There are also soy options that reduce the risk of reflux. And, there are the mainstay, regular formulas. There is a variation to the cost, and your doctor may recommend a brand depending on your particular situation.

When you are on the go, putting the correct amount of the powder into the bottle before you leave and taking a water bottle will make it much quicker if your baby is hungry when you didn't expect. If you have a refrigerated pre-mixed solution, just like when you take your lunch someplace, there are "cooler sleeves" (like for a cold drink) that will help keep your formula at the correct temperature until your little one needs to eat.

6. Pacifier

Get one. Even if you swear you won't be needing one, you might. There are a ton to choose from in many shapes, some that are shaped like a nipple while others are designed like a flat spoon. A pacifier can help when nothing else does and you can discontinue using it at any time should you decide to do so.

7. Diaper Bag

You will want to get something to carry baby supplies when you go out. It can be a traditional diaper bag, a backpack or even a plain canvas bag. Lots of things are required - diapers, whips, bottles, formula, pacifiers, a change of clothes (you'd be surprised), a rattle or colorful soft book they can hold and more - when taking your baby, so be prepared.

8. Co-Sleeper or Bassinet

Some moms opt to use a bassinet rather than a crib for the first month or two. It's more compact so it can fit in your room if you plan to co-sleep with your little one. It has a smaller sleeping area, too, which tends to make babies feel more secure. Plus, most are portable so you can take it with you when you take baby to visit family, friends or wherever else you may wander.

You can find co-sleepers and bassinets with some really great features. Some vibrate and others have toy mobiles or sound built into them. Then there are the really basic, even old-fashioned set ups like straw baskets. These types are adorable but are often really flimsy so if you use one, don't let other children or animal around while your baby is in it.

9. Crib

Your baby will most likely spend a lot of time in her crib. A crib should last for several years. It should also be a good, safe and comfortable place that your little one will have plenty of sweet dreams.

Having a crib before you have your baby is a good idea, mostly because life will be much busier after the arrival. As far as having it set up, that can wait (though it's easier before baby comes home) and if you can't get one yet, that's fine, too. Lots of mothers want the crib set up simply to complete the look of the nursery which is understandable but not imperative. Oftentimes babies sleep in bassinets, cradles or even little sleepers before graduating to a crib.

You'll have oodles and gobs of options where cribs are concerned. In fact, so much so, if can be overwhelming. You might like some of the features available like space saving options where the bed is smaller and often folds or collapses. Convertible cribs are great too because they transition into toddler beds as your child grows. Cribs that allow for the mattress height to be adjusted are optimal because when they are small and not able to roll over, the mattress can be higher to make it less strenuous on your back.

Some features are not optional, however, such as crib slat width. This is to increase the safety (and small kids don't get their head stuck in between the bars). Safety is top priority, so check the crib for an updated certification; never use or buy an older crib that doesn't meet current safety standards.

10. Dresser

It's a good idea to have a place to store your baby's clothes. You can get one that is made specifically for the nursery or use an adult one. You can even restore an old one to fit your baby's room décor. If you do use one that's not nursery-specified, especially if you go with an older one, do be sure there is no lead based paint on it. Paint chips and babies put everything in their mouths so it could pose a real hazard.

11. Changing Table

Keeping baby safe and comfortable is the object of a changing table. It will also be more convenient for you. Although you can certainly make your own, changing tables that are designated for baby's use are equipped with guard features (to help discourage rolling over) and safety buckle-ins (because as they get older they get wiggly) so you will want to incorporate the same features on yours if make your own.

12. Rocking Chair

You may not think that a rocking chair is a must, but just wait until you've been up all night with a fussy little one. Rocking motions help lull babies to sleep and help soothe colicky bouts as well. You can find rocking chairs in all shapes and sizes and in all price ranges, too. Old wooden rockers are a traditional favorite but may not be quite as comfy as the new and improved kinds. Gliders are another option. You may even want a rocker in the family room and the nursery.

13. Baby Monitor

Baby monitors take guess work out of it all. Is baby asleep? Is she fussing or is she entertaining herself? Has she spun herself from the top of the crib to the bottom? You don't have to wonder when you have a baby monitoring system in place.

A monitor is a device that acts as an intercom from baby's room to your room or wherever you choose to take the receiver. You can get really fancy (and expensive) ones that reach far distances so you can do yard work and still listen in on your little one. You can also get less expensive models that may suit your needs just as well. Whichever you use, it's advisable to get one. It's an amazing way to keep an ear on baby.

Most monitors now are promoted that you can have a camera and remote device (some even connecting to your smart phone) to see the baby. This eliminates disturbing their sleep by opening the door just to check on them. You can see how the baby is sleeping, hands thrown above his head or even sucking her thumb and self-soothing. The price of these monitors has really dropped in recent years, and is a good investment.

Some monitors now are devices that sit in the crib with your infant and monitor breathing habits, so you know if something changes with your child almost instantly. As infants don't "compensate" when something is wrong like the adult body does, things can happen very quickly. These devices can be expensive, but can provide the added sense of security that there's another set of "eyes" helping to watch your child.

14. Thermostat

It's important to keep your baby's room comfortable. She can't tell you if she's hot or cold so rather than having you guess, simply get a thermostat that you can place in her room. It's common to keep the nursery too extreme, too cold in the summer or too warm in the winter. Nothing could be more miserable for a little one who can't let you know so, a thermostat is definitely a cool choice. (Note that some of the fancy monitors also have this capability, so you may spend a little more for the visual monitor, but get more features, too.)

15. Nightlight

You'll want to weigh whether you want a nightlight or not. They are nice to have when you come at night to collect your fussing baby. But then again, baby's natural sleep rhythm is set up to sleep when it's dark. It's called the circadian rhythm and that is something you don't want to disturb. So, just like everything else is that concerns your child, it's your call. You may find that a night light outside the door to the baby's room provides enough ambient light into the doorway - so it's a matter of placement, too.

16. Humidifier/Vaporizer

When your baby gets stuffy, you'll want to have a humidifier or vaporizer handy. What's the difference? A humidifier creates a cool mist by using a fan while a vaporizer heats the water until hot steam is produced. Both mist the air so babies breathe better. Humidifiers are preferred by most because they don't get hot. It also depends on your climate as if you reside in a more humid, tropical climate, you likely won't need to consider this option like you would in areas that have dry or cold seasons.

17. Digital Ear Thermometers

Gone are the days when you had to take baby's temperature with a thermometer under an arm pit or in a very uncomfortable way for the baby. By simply placing the newer digital devices at the opening of her ear, you'll be able to squeeze the lever and her temperature will digitally display. Ask your doctor if there's a brand he or she prefers, as some devices may be more accurate than others or take better readings faster — both of which are important on a fussy uncomfortable little one.

18. Carriers

Infant seats allow you to take you little one around. They can often be used for the baby to sit for her feeding once she starts eating solids if you aren't into using a highchair. Some babies love their carriers so much, they prefer to sleep in them (which is fantastic at a fussy nap time), That's really not suggested, but it shows how comfy they can be.

19. Strollers

If you are going to take your little one out where you'll be doing much walking, you'll certainly want to have a stroller where she can sit or even lay while you are walking. Strollers come in all shapes and sizes as well as prices.

You can get very simple, inexpensive, fold-up types for short trips (but know they are sometimes difficult to steer and not all that comfortable). There are strollers designed for handling rough terrain with ease (while you jog or walk fast, for instance) and are luxurious for baby as well. There are even strollers designed to help you while shopping, with compartments for your keys and phone, purses or purchases.

20. Baby Portable Plays paces

Pack-and-play options let you take a little break (like your own run to the potty). They "contain" your baby as well as her toys and can be used for naps, too. They are especially great for trips. You can also get baby fences and baby gates to block off areas of your house, thus creating a play space, but know that once he starts walking, these may not be as secure as a space designed for a small child and toddler.

21. Bathtub

When it comes to bath time for baby, it can be a slippery task. A plastic baby tub makes bathing your baby much easier and safer, too. You can also use a large "baby sponge" that goes into the bathtub on which she can lay or you can opt to just use a wet cloth while she's on the changing table. Once baby gets bigger and can somewhat sit, there are devices that will help hold her in place in the home's bathtub. But remember, baby's have sensitive skin and don't necessarily need a bath every day - that dries their skin. Talk to your doctor about how often to give your baby a bath.

No matter which you choose, never ever leave your baby unattended.

22. Baby Nail Clippers

Most moms are scared to death to clip their baby's finger and toe nails at first but after a few rounds of hang-nail or baby scratching herself (and Mommy), the hesitation is over. Be sure to use one specifically designed for an infant as it doesn't need to be as sharp as an adult's clippers and has rounded ends so you don't accidentally poke your baby if she moves.

23. Toiletries

There will be a number of toiletries you'll want to have, like bath soap, shampoo and lotion. Be sure to get the baby-safe ones and don't use your own or even those designed for older children. Many parents are opting for organic blends because even though the baby brands are approved, they still may contain unwanted substances. Cotton swabs, diaper rash remedies and baby wash cloths are also on this list.

24. Bibs

Bibs are a must, even before baby is eating solid foods as they help protect her clothes from bottle overflow and spit-up. For catching that dripping milk, usually cloth bibs are best so it doesn't just roll onto your lap or clothing. When she is old enough to eat, you might consider the wipe-off ones that are made from vinyl.

25. Blankets

Babies need plenty of blankets. You will probably want to get at least one in light, medium and heavy weights. Remember to look for soft ones that don't scratch her sensitive skin.

Also, remember that having these laying the baby's crib isn't always the best choice. If you use them to bundle him while holding or swaddling, that's different than a blanket laying next to a sleeping child, where it can get tangled or cause discomfort or something worse to happen.

Other Innovative Solutions

The baby market is huge. It is estimated that the baby industry should rise to all all-time $66.8 billion dollar high by 2017. Diapers make up about 66% of the sales, but what constitutes for the rest of it? Baby stuff!

Sure, there are lots of things you need for your baby. Some are imperative. Then there are things that you don't need, you just want. But the clincher comes down to the things we purchase and don't even want or use.

Slap a cute little chubby cheek baby photo on a product, and sales increase. New mothers are the worst at buying stuff. You simply *must* have any gadget that promises to make your life easier and who can really blame you? But, just heed the warning and know that buyer's remorse runs thick among new moms.

That having been said, there are some really awesome new innovative products out and even more expected soon.

Breeza 4-in-1 Baby Bottle Washer: For about $250, you can get this hot machine that cleans and sterilizes bottles, binkies and more. The best thing about it is that you no longer have to scald your hands to wash bottles nor do you have to put them in the dishwasher with your pots and pans.

- **Vibrating Infant Seats:** These are a must for most moms. They have a dial where you can vary the degree of vibration and usually come with a mobile and music, too. Some even bounce. Great to have in a secure spot while you are making a meal or cleaning a room (and helps encourage napping, too).

- **Diaper Genies:** This device keeps dirty and wet used diapers in an airtight container so they don't stink up the changing area. There are a wide variety of options and features, but the airtight feature is the best! If you are planning on having other children, so this baby will be a toddler when you have the next child, invest in one with a "locking" lid... just a tip that it is money well spent for future exploration prevention.

- **Boppy Pillows:** These pillows are perfect to hold your baby in snugly while she nurses. They also can be used as she learns to sit up or he takes some tummy time once he's old enough to hold up his head.

- **Baby Sling:** How did mothers ever get along without these? Simply slide the sling over your head for hands-free carrying. They are available in a myriad of styles and price ranges. There was a concern about some brands that tend to cuddle the baby in a compromising position that could lead to suffocation. The main thing is to always be aware of your baby and to realize the sling is not a babysitter, just a helping hand.

- **Baby Swing:** Again, how did parents live without baby swings? Actually, not many have. Way back in the day, mothers found ways to tie cradles to trees in order to swing them. You'll find basic models, electric styles, battery operated ones, ones that play music (do make sure it can be turned off or down as a few models can't be) and ones that do all sorts of fancy thing. Some even have different speed features that are useful as your child grows and may need a more noticeable rock as they get older.

- **4Moms High Chair:** This highchair features a magnetic tray that pops right on and off. The dinnerware has magnetic bases so they stick to the tray.

- **EPZP Happy Mat:** This one will be of more interest as your baby gets a little older and begins that ever-so-sloppy stage of learning to feed herself. It's a silicone mat with a plate and bowl built right in. It's no slip and no slide…genius.

Baby Basics

"Life doesn't come with a manual. It comes with a mother."

- Author Unknown

It would be nice if babies came with instruction manuals. But, they don't. There are some great books that will help school you, this being one of them. You can also learn a lot from friends and family members (yes, even your mother-in-law). If you are still jittery, you can sign up for a class that will actually go through the motions of things like changing diapers and bathing baby. Chances are the material below will give you a good feel for it and the rest, you'll be able to wing just fine because that's what mothers do.

Diaper Duty

It is estimated that a given baby receives 7,300 diaper changes by her second birthday. And guess what? You'll be the one doing most of them. I'd say it's time to learn how!

Cloth diapers versus. Disposable

It's an age old question. Well, not really. Our ancestors used anything from milkweed leaves to animal pelts when diapering their young. Disposable diapers were invented in 1946 by a housewife and mother. The first version was merely a cloth diaper inserted into a plastic shower curtain. It wasn't until the 80's and 90's when they were perfected with new technology.

How to diaper

The type of diaper you choose to use will determine the steps you will need to take to change them. For that reason, this section is divided into two sections, cloth and disposables.

On a side note, you really might want to teach your partner to do this, too. Remember, having a baby is a joint effort and if you just take over and change the baby every single time, never presenting an opportunity to help, you probably won't get any.

Disposables

This method is only a suggestion to get you started. After you get the hang of it, you'll have your own system down. But, in the meantime, here is a step-by-step outline you can follow.

1. Be sure your hands are clean. This can be done with soap and water, hand sanitizer or diaper wipe. Some frown on sanitizers recently due to some unwanted chemicals in them so do your homework and choose what works best for you.

2. Cover a comfortable and safe changing area with a clean towel, sheet or blanket. If you are using a changing table, that's even better because the cover on the cushion is washable.

3. Be sure you have everything you need: a diaper, wipes or a damp cloth, diaper rash cream or powder if applicable, something to throw the dirty diaper in and your baby, of course. You don't want to realize you forgot something because especially if you are using a changing table that's high, you won't want to leave your baby unattended (even strapped to the table). Have the clean diaper already open and within quick reach of the changing area (it's hard to open with one hand as your other one stays on your baby's tummy so they don't wiggle too much on the changing table).

4. Take the dirty diaper off your baby. Watch for the sticky tabs so they don't stick to your baby. You can basically scoop the poop away with the diaper for the most part. Also, be careful not to get poop on his or her genitals if it can be helped as you remove the dirty diaper and place it to the side. Clean her, making sure you clean her with her bottom lifted off the table or cushion after you've removed the dirty diaper so you don't have a second dirty spot. (You can hold her legs up with one hand as you wipe her with the other.) Apply diaper cream, if needed.

5. Throw the dirty diaper in a genie, the trash.

6. Put the new diaper under the baby halfway, so that the back half with the tabs on it is under her back and bottom.

7. Pull the front part of the diaper up high, to just below the umbilical cord or higher if it has fallen off. If you have a boy, you may want to point his penis down or at least make sure the diaper is well above it or the diaper may leak — even if you've bought gender-specific diapers.

8. Make sure the diaper is not all bunched up in the middle or at the leg holes, making it uncomfortable.

9. Unfasten the tabs and adhere the top part of the diaper to the bottom, snug but not too tight.

10. Give her a "once over" to make sure no tape is sticking to her and that there's nothing else out of place.

Now you're ready to dress her and by all means, wash your hands!

Cloth Diapers

Changing a baby into and out of a cloth diaper is the same as with a disposable with a few minor switches. First, you will use a folded cloth diaper rather than a disposable one, of course. Just as with a disposable, the largest half goes in the back. You may opt to put a disposable liner between her and the diaper. The only other change is that you use diaper pins to secure the diaper.

Here's one method of folding a cloth diaper:

Lay the diaper completely open on a flat surface. You can double the thickness by adding a second diaper that will go right on top (and they will be folded as if they were one).

With the upper right corner not moving, fold the lower left third diagonally. Do the same for the other side. The bottom should not be to a point but should have a few inches of flat surface.

Bring the bottom of the diaper one-third of the way up.

There you have it…a folded diaper!

Clothes

Here's a reality check on those sweet little outfits you can't wait to put on your baby. Remember when you were a little girl and used to dress up your baby dolls? Sorry to say, but dressing your real live doll will doubtfully be anything like that.

She'll probably put up a fuss and try to "help." But, it's lots of fun when it's done, seeing her in an adorable little outfit… until she poops, that is, and starts to cry. If you're lucky, though, you'll snap a picture before-hand. Oh, and one more thing: you are much more likely to enjoy the cute little clothes than she is.

Of course you'll want to have some fancy dresses or handsome little suits for photos and special occasions, but comfy and practical clothing are what you'll want to have the most of. She'll thank you for that one day - and it makes washing the laundry easier for parents!

As tempting as it is to collect itty-bitty outfits throughout your pregnancy, you might want to hold off on newborn sizes. Many babies are too big for them at birth. Others stay in them for a while. Still some wear preemie sizes and grow into the newborn size. It's helpful to know how large or small your little one will run before getting a lot of clothes in one size. Keeping the tags intact and saving the receipt is a great idea in case you need to return anything.

Newborn size is about 5-9 pounds. Preemie is five pounds and under. But this doesn't match to how they label sizes! For babies before they start walking, size 0-3 is 9-13 pounds. Size 3-6 is generally 13-17 pounds and 6-9 months is 17-20.

Here is an estimate of the clothes your little one will need the first month in whichever sizes are appropriate (and sometimes that will entail two sizes):

- **Shirts and T-Shirts:** 4-6, long or short sleeved, depending on the weather and temperature of your home

- **Onesies:** 7-8, short or long sleeved (or both)

- **Infant Gowns**: 3-4, recommended by the American Academy of Pediatrics (AAP) when used instead of a blanket, sheet or other covering

- **Stretch (Sleeper) Pajamas:** 3-6, also recommended by the AAP

- **Pants and Leggings:** 3-4

- **Hats, Caps, Bonnets:** 1 or 2

- **Booties and Socks:** 6-10, you may need to change these as often as diapers

- **Blanket Sleepers:** 3-4, again, recommended by the AAP as an alternative to loose bedding that can increase the risk of SIDS (Sudden Death Syndrome)

Here are some helpful hints concerning your baby's clothing:

- Avoid clothing that fits too tightly around her neck.

- Watch for tags, zippers, hooks, etc. that can be uncomfortable.

- Be sure the fabric is comfortable on her skin.

- Wash her laundry separately in a mild, hypoallergenic detergent.

- Even newborns can choke on buttons, appliqués and decorations that come loose from clothing so always be aware.

Your Little One's Laundry

At first, you won't believe the amount of dirty laundry your baby can accumulate but as long as you keep a load going every day or so, it won't get as overwhelming as you may fear. Not only will you be washing her clothing but also the bedsheets, changing table covers and blankets as well. It is important to keep her laundry separate and to wash it separately — especially if you are using cloth diapers and laundering them at home. Baby laundry detergent is made for sensitive skin so it's a must and if your little one has extra sensitive skin, you will want to go with the baby detergent for extra sensitive skin.

Healing at Home

Caring for your baby

Tending to your little one will come quite natural in many ways. But rest assured, there will be times that you will have questions. Not knowing everything certainly does not make you an inadequate mother. Even the best moms don't know it all and neither do they pretend to know everything. They ask, research and listen to others. The willingness to learn is the mark of a wise and wonderful mother.

Bonding

Bonding is the process of creating a mutual emotional and psychological closeness between you and your baby. It usually begins during pregnancy and often blossoms just minutes after your baby is born. You look into her eyes and the two of you are instantly bonded. But, that doesn't always happen and don't feel bad if it doesn't. It doesn't mean you don't love your baby or that she doesn't love you. Here are some factors that can delay bonding:

- **Cesarean Section, Tuba Ligation or other Surgery.** If you have required medication during childbirth, you may wake up groggy. You may even be on medication for a few days to a week. This very well may inhibit the bonding process so just be patient.

- **Stress.** If you are anxious and stressed, your body may not adequately pick up the signals from your brain that have to do with bonding. The more you relax, the more likely it is that bonding will naturally happen.

- **Pressure.** A watched pot is slow to boil. If you are overly fixated on the moment bonding will take place, you may be putting too much pressure on yourself and your little one.

- **Medical Issues.** If you or your baby have medical complications such as a premature birth or birth defect, she may spend much or all of the first days in an incubator. While there will be no doubt that you intensely love your baby, actual bonding may take longer to actually occur.

If you are finding that you and your baby are not bonded or not as closely as you want to be, you might find these things helpful:

- **Breastfeeding.** Breastfeeding requires you and your little one to be attached physically so it's the ultimate time to enhance your emotional bond as well. If you aren't breastfeeding, try feeding her from the bottle as if you are breastfeeding so that you always hold and never prop the bottle and you hold her as closely as you would if nursing her.

- **De-stress.** Do all that you can to unwind. Take hot bubble baths. Go for strolls with your infant. Enlist help so that you are not overly tired. Anything and everything that you can do to get rid of bottled up stress and anxiety is helpful.

- **Communicate.** Take time during diaper changes, feedings and rocking to talk to your baby as if she is your best friend.

Secure Attachment vs. Bonding

Although there are many similarities between secure attachment and bonding, they are two different things. Secure attachment is the feeling of trust and well-being that your baby develops through the emotional links with you. It greatly determines how well your baby will do in life. Bonding is the physical and emotional the two of you have that is often acquired and communicated during activities such as feedings.

Secure attachment is when your baby feels loved, understood and secure. In a study published on the Princeton University website, four in ten children lack strong secure attachment bonds. The lack of security often gives way to behavioral and educational issues.

To ensure that your baby is developing secure attachment bonds that will give her the ability to live life on life's terms, take every opportunity you can to assure her emotionally. Spend as much time as you can with her, not just doing but "being" with her as she does little activities. You will soon find that she is receiving that which you are giving and the effects will be life-long.

Holding and Handling Your Baby

You might be surprised to learn how many mothers and fathers are apprehensive to hold their newborn infant. And rightly so. Because your little one's neck muscles are not yet able to support her head, you will need to support her neck. This fact alone can make the experience unnerving but don't worry, once you get the hang of it, it's a piece of cake.

Here are step-by-step instructions on how to hold your baby, cradle-style:

1. Rest her head comfortably on your chest with your hand your hand slid under her bottom to give her neck support.

2. In a gentle, smooth motion, move her head to the bend in your arm so that her neck is supported.

3. Cradle your baby and take the opportunity to communicate with her through eye-to-eye contact and words as well.

4. Avoid handing her to someone else in the upright position as she cannot hold her head straight - it's the heaviest part of her

body at this point. Always let them slide their arms under yours to lift the baby and change the person holding her.

Soothing and Comforting Your Little One

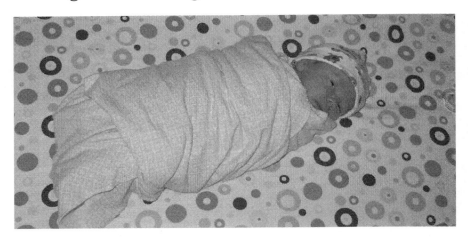

When baby isn't happy, nobody's happy. A fussy baby not only makes herself miserable but makes everyone else in the household miserable as well. In the book, "The Happiest Baby on the Block", the author, Harvey Karp, M.D., has some brilliant and very effective suggestions to help calm and sooth your itty bitty, most notably, the Five "S's".

Here are some things you might want to try:

1. **Swaddle.** Swaddling is snugly wrapping your baby to resemble the womb in which she came from. Simply use a large blanket to wrap your baby's body inside, carefully never including her head, just her body. Keep her arms straight to her side yet allow her hips to be loose and limber. Make sure she isn't too hot and that she doesn't stay swaddled all day

long. This method helps promote sleep and discourages startling and fussiness.

2. **(Back) Sleeping.** Babies tend to balk at being on their backs. But, due to SIDS, medical professionals do not recommended that your baby sleep on her side or tummy. Swaddling helps with this back sleeping position.

3. **Shush.** Funny but as quiet as mom's love to keep the house when trying to get their little ones to sleep, total silence is generally not conducive to sleep. Did you know that the womb makes a noise that is actually louder than a vacuum cleaner? Keeping noise at a low level "shush" is usually much more effective than no noise at all and now we know why. That's why some people get white noise machines for a baby's room, to make it as similar to the womb as possible (and it dims out any other background noise as your cook, clean and talk on the phone).

4. **Swing.** Ahhh… the swing. As it was mentioned in the Top 25 list, if you don't have one, get one. Most mothers swear by them. You can get one that is made to cradle tiny ones and grows with them into a seat for their legs. You can also swing your baby yourself by swaying gently just as a swing does…back and forth…back and forth.

5. **Suck.** It's a natural born instinct for a baby to suck. It actually stems from a need to survive, a brain thing. So give her what she craves. She should have something to suck, be it a pacifier, a teething ring, her thumb, a bottle or your breast at mealtime.

Skin Care 101

Baby's skin has a much different make up than adult skin does. It is soft and supple, full of hyaluronic acid. Adults envy the plump, silky-smooth skin and often thing that frequent bathing your entire baby (not just his diaper area) is the way to keep it so perfect — but that's not the case so check the area on bathing later in this chapter. And not only is baby's skin beautiful to behold, it is very sensitive as well.

Even normal baby skin is prone to rashes such as diaper rash and heat rash, even yeast rashes. If your little one has a patch of small to large red bumps, chances are good that he has one or the other. It can be hard to tell the difference between diaper and heat rash. Diaper rash tends to affect the area where urine or poop may come in contact with his skin whereas heat rash generally covers a larger area. If you are in doubt, his pediatrician may want to take a look at it.

Creams can be used to help soothe rashes. There are many on the market. Your baby's pediatrician can recommend one if you are in doubt as to which is best.

Some babies have extremely sensitive skin. If yours does, you will want to take all measures possible to prevent irritation. Keeping baby lotion on her skin is a good idea. If you do so though, be sure to let her skin breathe for periods of time without lotion or cream on it.

It's important to wash baby and her laundry in soap that is especially made for sensitive baby skin. Don't confuse baby and adult products. Just because an adult bath or laundry soap is for sensitive skin doesn't make it fit for your baby.

Lotions, powders, creams: everything must be for sensitive skin. Many products on the market are for baby's sensitive skin and may be labeled as non-irritant, but there are certain ingredients that may still be integrated in these mass-produced baby care products. For that reason, organic solutions are usually best. Look for a good, all-natural brand that makes a number of products for baby that most tolerate well.

You may also find that baby sheets, blankets, clothes and so forth irritate her skin. You can find organic blends that are made for sensitive, allergy-prone skin. Also consider the clothing you are wearing since you may hold her to your shoulder, thus, laying her head on your shirt.

Baby eczema, psoriasis and dermatitis are medical skin conditions that can occur with babies. It is best to see her pediatrician if you suspect she has one of these conditions. They are not life-threatening, so don't worry, but they are uncomfortable and each requires a different remedy so best to get a proper diagnosis.

Rashes and skin irritations can be a sign of a more serious condition. Although this is generally not the case, it is wise to check any suspicious places out and if you think it could be problematic, certainly check with your pediatrician. Here are a few ailments with skin bumps and irritations:

- Irritations, especially when accompanied by extremely soft or hard skin, can indicate an internal disease.

- Warts are not uncommon on babies and can be a sign of a viral disease.

- Candida is a condition that is known to affect babies. White bumps in your baby's mouth or a shiny red rash in her diaper area can be a tell-tale sign.

- Impetigo is a fairly common childhood condition. It is characterized by a red, moist rash that fill with puss, burst and turn yellow and crusty.

Safety Concerns

Childproofing Your Home

The time to start baby-proofing your home is while you are still pregnant. There are things that need to be done prior to bringing your little one home. Plus, you will have more time sooner rather than later.

Here is a list of some of the things you will want to do:

Before Baby:

- Invest in a top-quality air purifier and keep it running. Babies are susceptible to dust, dander, mold and impurities.

- Purchase a humidifier. If you end up needing one once your baby is born, it will no doubt be in the wee hours of the night. Best to prepare beforehand.

- Invest in a white noise machine. Babies tend to sleep better when there is a gentle bit of soothing noise.

- Declare your home a smoke-free zone if it's not already. Even secondhand smoke on clothing can harm your baby.

- Consider a water purification system that cleans the water you use to bathe your baby or use to make formula for bottles. Toxins from water sources do soak through the skin, especially baby's skin, and babies are more susceptible to things in a public water supply that adults can normally process.

After Baby (or before if you are able to):

- Be sure there are NO items in the crib.

- Secure any loose items that could cause choking such as small toys belonging to older siblings

- Cover electrical plugs and implement safety covers on outlets. Secure dangling and loose cords.

- Install door stops so doors can't slam shut.

- Install window locks.

- Secure dangling shade or min-blind cords.

- Vacuum and sweep the floors and continue to do so regularly.

- Secure bookshelves, TV stands, entertainment centers, etc.

- Install baby gates, especially across stair entrances and kitchen areas.

- Install fire and monoxide alarms. Be sure to have a fire extinguisher in the garage and kitchen at the very least.

- Secure heating vents and cold air returns.

- Secure or remove all firearms from the home.

- Check for any sources of lead paint.

- Secure all knives, plastic bags and sharp cooking utensils.

- Secure all medications.

- Lock away all cleaning supplies, detergents, fire extinguishers, paint, etc.

- Secure all appliances.

- Put locking tabs on cabinets and drawers. You can leave one drawer and/or cabinet in the kitchen for baby to access toys while you cook.

- When cooking, use back burners and keep handles turned inward.

- Install a toilet seat lock.

- Install a ground fault circuit interrupt.

- Throw rugs down on hard surfaces such as the bathroom floor.

- Keep razors, shaving creams and so forth away from baby's reach, especially on bathtub ledge and bathroom sinks.

- Secure areas underneath all the beds.

- Secure the fireplace or wood burning stove. Install a wrap-around gate if need be.

- Remove all tablecloths and runners.

- Move alcohol to upper cabinets.

- Never leave your purse, jewelry or tobacco products within reach and be sure other family members and guests don't either.

Travel

Since it is impossible to ensure that all hotels and relatives homes are baby proofed, the best rule of thumb is to bring your own play area such as a pack-and-play for safe time out of your arms or if your child is older, bring a fold up gate where you can create a safe environment.

Safety Labels

Never assume that because a product is advertised safe for your baby that is truly is. Thousands of items are recalled every year. Periodically check the recall list on products you purchase and also, be sure that the way in which you are using the items doesn't allow for error. A highchair may be perfectly safe and certified as such but if you scoot it too close to your table and your child can push the table edge with her feet, she can possibly tip the high chair backwards. You don't have to be paranoid, but do be alert and aware.

Making a Splash: Bath Time for Baby

Baby's bath time can be a pleasant, fun and relaxing experience for both you and your baby. Or, it can be a nightmare and can be dangerous as well. With a little loving care and knowledge, you can make it a time to treasure.

When to start bathing baby

Until your baby's umbilical cord falls off and heals, you will want to give her sponge or wash cloth baths. Then, anytime you feel the two of you are ready is fine to start tub baths.

The tub

When your little one is tiny, you can use a baby tub that has a contoured shape that will secure her above the water and keep her at the right angle for bathing. Or, you can opt for an inside the tub sling that keeps her in place and prevents sliding. Bath seats are discouraged as they have been known to tip over.

Temperature

Lukewarm water is the best for baby. Check the temperature prior to placing her into the bath. You can use your elbow to gage if the water is too hot, too cold or just right. Don't forget to continually check it to be sure it hasn't cooled off too much as bath time shouldn't be a long experience for your little one at this age. You can get cute rubber ducks and other bath toys that give a temperature reading but never completely rely on them.

Bath schedule

Most infants don't need to be bathed every single day. Especially if during the wintertime or you live in a dry climate, your baby's skin will become dry and likely have an outbreak of one of the skin rashes mentioned earlier. Two to three times a week should be sufficient for a formal bathing though you can clean her face and diaper area as needed.

The time of day you bathe her is a matter of personal preference. Many moms like to have bath time just before bedtime because they find it calms and soothes baby and gets her ready for a good night's sleep. Others find quite the contrary, so see what works best for your little one.

Choosing bath products

Products that are baby-specific are the best. You will need soap, shampoo and lotion as well. Many products designed for babies still have perfume and dyes in them and other unwanted ingredients too like sulfates. Organic bath products are a good choice because you will not find chemicals, dyes or even GMO's in them.

Baby hair care

It isn't necessary to shampoo your babe's hair with each bath. You can usually do so once a week unless it appears or smells dirty. You do want to be sure to use a washcloth when you wash it to help prevent "cradle cap" (which is the build- up of dead skin, and the washcloth helps wash away those cells).

Keeping baby safe while bathing

Never turn your head or let go of your baby for even just a second. Disaster can strike in an instant. Before the bath, make sure you have all her bath necessity items within arm's reach. When the bath is over, quickly and gently wrap her up and be careful, wet babies are wiggly and slippery.

Tub tips

- Lower the setting on your water heater to 120 degrees and consider putting a baby-lock on your faucets.

- Use a cover over the spout to prevent her from hitting her head on it.

- Empty the tub immediately after use.

- Use a non-skid baby mat.

- If your baby hates bath time, continue to work on helping her like it but cut the time short and never force the issue.

- Usually between 7-9 months is when little ones transition to the big tub. Be sure you have anti-slip measures in place and faucets covered.

- If baby pees, bath time is over. Rinse her off after you have gotten her out of the tainted water.

Safety Matters: Baby's First-Aid Kit

It is imperative to assemble a first-aid kit specifically for your little one. Babies require different emergency items that adults do. You will want to have one in the house, one in the car and one to take along with you when traveling. You can find locking boxes that will securely house the items in it so the first-aid kit itself doesn't become a danger. You'll also want to learn infant CPR as it's different than what's performed on adults (and gives you instruction on what to do if your baby is choking).

You will want to include:

- Cotton swabs

- Cotton balls

- Bandages, tape and pads

- Band-aides

- Sterile gauze bandages and tape

- Surgical tape

- Digital thermometer

- Scissors

- Tweezers

- Medicine dropper

- Flashlight (with back-up batteries)

- Blankets

- Antibiotic ointment

- Antiseptic solution

- Burn ointment

- Calamine lotion or equivalent

- 1% or less hydrocortisone ointment

- Petroleum jelly

- Distilled water

- Soap

- Baby pain reliever as recommended by pediatrician

- Antihistamine and Decongestant (check with pediatrician)

- Any medicines required specifically for your baby

- Heimlich maneuver and CPR instructions

- Sterile hand wipes

- Emergency phone numbers

- Poison kit

Sudden Infant Death Syndrome (SIDS): Awareness and Prevention

The heart-wrenching pain of losing a child is something no parent should have to go through. Sadly, though, it does happen all too often. It is estimated that about 1,500 infants die each year in the United States alone, according to statistics obtained from the Centers of Disease Control and Prevention.

Sudden Infant Death Syndrome, or SIDS, is the name given when a seemingly healthy infant dies with no explanation. It is often referred to as "crib death". SIDS generally happens during the night and research has found that SIDS is greatly reduced when babies are on their back to sleep.

The cause of the syndrome is not known. But, there are factors that seem to follow suit to indicate that a portion of the babies' brains are abnormal, a very important section that is responsible for breathing and wakening.

Some factors that are thought to play a part of SIDS are:

- Premature or low birth weight

- Brain abnormalities

- Infection of the respiratory system

- Sleeping on side or tummy

- Sleeping on an overly soft surface

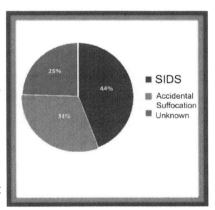

- Sharing a sleeping space with parent or parents

- Being a male

- Being 2-3 months of age

- Family history of SIDS

- Smokey environment

- A mother under the age of 20

- A mother who smokes cigarettes, takes drugs or drinks alcohol

- Lack of proper prenatal care

Preventative measures

- Always place your baby on her back to sleep.

- If she wakes up in the night, be sure to place her back on her back when you put her back down.

- If someone else puts your baby to bed, be sure to double-check that they put her properly on her back.

- Make sure there are no extra blankets in the bed. Blanket or sleeper pajamas are a much better alternative.

- Be sure there are no toys, pillows or even crib bumper pads in the bed with your baby.

- Keep pets and younger children out of the baby's nursery or sleeping quarters.

- Keep the baby's room an average temperature, not too hot nor too cold.

- Be sure the baby sleeps alone, without toys or blankets in the bed.

- Give your baby a pacifier if she will take one as it has been proven to help reduce the risk of SIDS.

- Avoid baby monitors and other such devices that could pose a possible problem.

- Breastfed babies are at less risk than bottle-fed ones so breast feeding your little one is advised.

Chapter Takeaways

1. There are pros and cons to both cloth and disposable diapers so your personal preference will play a big role in the decision but ultimately, it is baby who has the final word.

2. You need a baby first aid kit that is separate from an adult one.

3. Be sure to have all of your baby changing items before you start changing your baby.

4. Babies do not have to be bathed every day, and when you do, use lukewarm water.

5. Be sure to learn infant CPR.

The Early Feeding Frenzy

"Eat, poop…and repeat."

- Author Unknown

From the moment your baby enters the world, her life will be focused on food (at least for a while, that is). But that's a good thing. Not only is food sustaining, it is enjoyable and it's  comforting, too. Later on, eating will be social as well. Now is the time to be sure your baby learns a good, positive outlook on food and develops healthy eating habits as well.

If your baby is balking for food a lot and seems to not be getting full, you might check to be sure the flow of the nipple you are using is adequate if he is feeding by a bottle. Otherwise, you want to be sure your breast milk is filling him up by checking with your doctor as well as your baby's doctor.

Another consideration is that your little one's activity level uses calories so think about this when figuring how much he needs to eat. A very active baby burns more calories and may require a higher caloric intake. If your baby is not sleeping well at night, he may not be getting enough to eat.

Milk versus Formula

Breastfeeding

Breastfeeding is science, psychology and practicality working hand-in-hand. It's a beautiful blend. If you have chosen to breastfeed, congratulations. A blessing awaits you.

If you have chosen not to breastfeed or are not able to feed your baby this way, don't worry. Motherhood is about progress, not perfection. You can actually implement some of the benefits of breastfeeding into bottle feeding. So read on, whether you are breast or bottle feeding, take the meat and spit out the bones, so to speak.

Benefits

Breast milk has tons of antibiotics that can't be duplicated in formula. Breastfed babies tend to get less colds, ear infections, sinus conditions and other illnesses than formula-fed infants. Remember when we learned about how the hormones signal a mother's brain to love and bond? 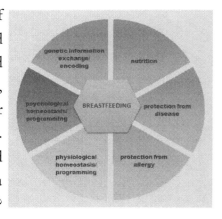 They also signal her body to produce milk.

Here are a few things you may not know about breastfeeding:

- A mother's milk changes daily to meet the nutritional requirements of her little one.

- The mother's brain is stimulated by breastfeeding. Some experts feel it causes her to become smarter.

- Breastfeeding encourages bonding.

- A baby's brain is also stimulated and nurtured by breastfeeding.

- Nursing releases the hormone oxytocin, which reduces activation of the amygdala and this, in turn, relieves stress.

How to Breastfeed

Ideally, your baby will easily latch onto your breast, the milk will flow and feeding your baby will be perfect. But nothing in life is guaranteed to be without a hitch and motherhood is no exception. Here is a step-by-step guide for breastfeeding should you need small adjustments:

1. Position your baby on her side, facing you so that her tummy is actually up against yours. You can prop her up with a pillow or special breastfeeding pillow. Hold her up to your breasts rather than vice versa.

2. With your thumb and fingers around your areola, slightly tilt your little one's head backwards and touch or tickle her lips with your nipple so that she opens her mouth.

3. By placing her lower jaw on first, you encourage her to scoop in your breast.

4. Now you can tilt her head forward so that her upper jaw is taking in your breast and nipple. No less than 1 ½ inches of the areola should be in her mouth.

5. For a **cradle hold** while nursing, lay your babe positioned onto your forearm with her head in the crook of your arm while you give support to her bottom from your free hand. You can now pull her close so that the two of you are belly-to-belly.

6. Another holding style is called the **football**. This method is extremely helpful if you have had a C-section. Simply lay your baby on a pillow that is tucked near your side. Now, rest your arm on the pillow while bringing your baby's mouth to your breast as you support her head.

7. Yet another holding method is **side-lying**. Just lie on the side that you will be feeding from and place your head on a pillow while holding your little one close to you. Again, support her bottom and use your free hand to unite baby's mouth and your breast.

Troubleshooting Breast Feeding

If your little one is having trouble catching on or simply doesn't like to breastfeed, there are a few things you can do.

- Be sure she is latching on well. If not, work with her until she does.

- Make sure you are relaxed and are presenting a stress-free nursing session.

- Consult a club of breastfeeding mothers online, in person or on the phone.

- Be sure you are drinking enough water.

- Check into teas and other solutions that stimulate breast milk production if you feel your milk supply is low.

- Talk to her pediatrician if the problem persists.

How Long to Breast Feed

Some babies nurse for only days or weeks while others nurse for years. Only you can really determine the length of time that's best for both you and your baby. If you can and your little one cooperates, it's good to go at least six months. Cow's milk isn't recommended until one year of age, so if you can breastfeed until then, even better.

Here are some signs that your baby is ready to be weaned or that you are ready to wean her:

- She cuts back on length of time she feeds and the frequency of feeding.

- You need to take medicine or have a medical procedure that is not conducive to nursing.

- You or she is just not "feeling it".

- She is biting beyond what you can (or should) bear.

Pumping Breast Milk

You may find that the need arises to have a supply of breast milk for your baby if you are going back to work or planning to leave her with a sitter, friend or family member. Pumping is also sometimes recommended to produce more milk if you are having trouble in that area.

You can purchase a pump online, at most any store that carries baby items or hospitals sometimes sell or rent them. Some insurance companies contribute all or part of the cost, so be sure to check that out prior to getting one in case there are any specific guidelines.

Once you secure a pump, here are some helpful hints:

- Follow the instructions on the pump you choose as the instructions vary.

- Many women say they get the best results in the morning hours.

- If you are pumping and breastfeeding, it is good to wait 30 minutes to an hour after feeding or no less than one hour before feeding so as not to diminish your supply.

- If your baby is wanting to nurse right after you have pumped, let her. She may have to work harder and wait longer but no harm done.

- If you are pumping and not breastfeeding, expect to pump about 10 times per day.

Bottle Feeding Basics

The way in which you hold your baby to take her bottle can be a modified version of the above methods of breastfeeding. There are additional things to take into consideration when bottle feeding, too.

To Sterilize or Not to Sterilize

You will need to sterilize new nipples, bottles, pacifiers and bottle rings. To do so, put them in a pot of boiling water for five minutes. Then, allow them to air dry on a fresh, clean towel. Then, put them through the dishwasher or wash them in hot, soapy water and again, air dry on a clean towel.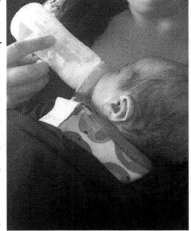

It isn't deemed necessary to continue to sterilize them after each use unless you feel better doing so. If you have well water, though, you may want to consider it or if you live in an area with questionable quality water supply (and, sadly, this is becoming the norm).

Something worth researching is the advantages of using glass or BPA-free bottles as plastic ones are made with bisphenol A and other chemicals that actually release toxins when heated. That is certainly not a good thing when you baby ingests milk or formula from the bottles.

Types of Nipples

Silicone and latex are the basic choices when it comes to nipples. The difference is that silicone nipples tend to hold their shape and are firmer while latex ones are softer and more pliable.

As far as the shape goes, there are those that are the typical nipple shape and others that are specially shaped with orthodontics in mind, having a flatter "spoon-like" shape. You may have a preference, but your baby will most likely have one all her own.

There are differences in nipple flow, which changes for your baby's age group. In fact, different types allow the fluid to come out slower or faster. You can progressively work up to a larger flow as your little one grows. Most likely, he will begin to complain or you will note that he is having trouble getting enough milk at one time.

Formulas

There are a multitude of formulas as you will quickly learn if your baby is bottle fed, either totally or in part. There are regular blends, types for sensitive digestion, preemie kinds, regurgitated milk, formula with iron, formula without iron, organic formula and the list seems to never end. Chances are you will start out on a basic type and go from there. If your baby doesn't do well on it, then you will try different varieties. The exception is some mothers know from the start they want to go the natural, organic way. Yet even in the organics, there are many choices.

Always, always use purified water to make your baby's bottle. A good rule is not to assume all bottled and purified waters are alike. They aren't. You might even consider a filtration system for your home. They are not all alike either. It's best to do your homework on whichever way you are leaning and if you have not had your baby yet, there's no time like the present to research before things get way busy.

Burping the baby

The reason for burping your baby is to prevent bubbles in her tummy. Bubbles cause gas (causing pain) and can also instigate colic (an extreme case of gas). Burping also frees up a little  more space for her to hold more milk.

Most infants need to burp with each feeding, but if she doesn't then she doesn't. You will get to know your little one and how long she generally takes to produce a burp and what happens if she doesn't. If she is usually well if she doesn't burp during her feeding, don't worry too much about it. If she does lean toward having tummy trouble, you might make efforts as long as you need to in order to get her to bring up the gas through a burp or two. Breastfed babies tend to get less air during feeding so have the need to burp less frequently.

Method One

Hold your little one against your chest so that her chin is comfortably at rest on your shoulders. Gently pat or rub her back with one hand while supporting her neck with the other. Most babies do well with pats to their upper back while others do best with lower pats.

Method Two

Hold your baby up high on your shoulder so that your shoulder and her tummy are even. While supporting her head with one hand, gently rub and/or pat her on the back with the other hand.

Method Three

Yet another way is to hold your babe on your lap so that she is in a sitting position, facing down, away from you. While supporting her head with one hand, rub and pat with the other. You can use this same method with her laying across your legs while you are sitting.

Getting Bigger and Starting Solid Foods

Eating solids

The American Academy of Pediatrics recommends starting your baby on solid food between the ages of four to six months. This holds true ONLY when your little one can: sit upright, hold her

head up, is curious and alert, seems to be still hungry after drinking 8-10 breast-feedings or 32 ounces of formula and has mastered the movement of her tongue. Your pediatrician may have a different opinion entirely, so be sure to check.

Got Milk? Should Breast or Bottle Feeding Be Continued?

For a while, it will be more important that your baby gets her milk, be it breast or bottle, than it is for her to eat solids. It's generally advised to give her milk first thing in the morning and before or after her meals then again at bedtime. This schedule can be adjusted depending upon your baby, how old she is, her preference of eating solids or drinking milk and of course, the recommendation from her pediatrician.

An approximation of how much milk she should get is:

- 20-28 ounces of milk every 3-4 hours up to 9 months of age.

- 16-24 ounces of milk every 4-5 hours from ages 9-12 months.

Tentative Solids Schedule

Sometime around the age of one, your baby will most likely become very interested in eating solids. This is when you can start at least offering three meals a day and giving milk as a compliment to the meal rather than vice versa. Don't forget to take snapshots of those funny faces when your little tries a new food. Some types of food will end up on the floor and others will be devoured. It's always a hoot to see which will end up where.

Finger foods (like crackers, yogurt melts and baby puffs) are great for her to have as snacks. Not only are they yummy, they are actually good for her hand-mouth coordination, promoting finger dexterity. Teething biscuits will help soothe aching gums.

An estimate of the average amount of solids your baby should be getting is as follows:

- Two meals per day, 2-4 teaspoons when 4-6 months.

- Three meals per day, each meal the size of her fist, 7-12 months.

Tasty Tips

1. Be sure to wash your hands before preparing her food and clean her hands prior to eating.

2. Babies and toddlers are slobs when they eat. Don't fuss about it if she is or isn't. Have fun right along with her and take lots of cute pictures.

3. If she insists of feeding herself, let her. Just be sure if she isn't very successful at getting it in her mouth that you compensate for the loss.

Baby Bites

Here are some good solids to feed your baby:

- **Single grains.** From four to six months, single grain foods are optimal. Rice, oats and barley are some favorites. At nine months of age, your baby will most likely reach an all-time low in iron due to the depletion of what was stored up from the womb. Iron-fortified grain cereals can be chosen to help restore iron in her system. You may want to start out by adding plenty of breast milk or formula to the mix so that it's very thin. Gradually, you can try a thicker combination.

- **Pureed fruits, vegetables and meats.** At around four to eight months, fruits, veggies and meats can be offered. Your doctor may suggest that you give vegetables before fruit so she doesn't develop a sweet tooth that keeps her from liking non-sweet foods. Meats are usually the last of the three food types that are introduced.

- **Ground, mashed or chopped foods.** At approximately nine to twelve months, a new milestone is reached when your little one can actually have what you are having (providing it's nutritious and among the recommended foods and that you ground, mash or chop it well).

A Few Things to Keep in Mind

- There are many types of baby foods and you should read all labels carefully. Certified organic varieties do not contain chemicals or GMO's.

- It's a good idea to try one new food at a time and give it five days to a week before trying another one to see if she has any allergic reactions.

Foods to Avoid

- Honey (it can cause botulism if introduced too soon).

- Cow's Milk (until your pediatrician gives the go-ahead and even then, many moms are going with organic)

- Nuts, Popcorn, Dried Fruits, Raisins and Peanut Butter (these foods can cause choking and allergic reactions)

- Sugary Sweets

- Junk Foods

- Citrus (until her pediatrician says it's alright to try it as it is an allergy risk)

Homemade Baby Food Recipes

If you have the time and are up for it, making your baby's food is fun and rewarding. It's a good feeling to think that you made your baby's very first foods.

It can be healthier to make your own baby food, too. You can use fresher items like veggies straight from the produce stand or fruit from the tree in your own backyard. It's a good idea to opt for organic ingredients. Below you will find some great baby-tested and approved recipes.

Barley Baby-Style (4-6 months +)

- ¼ cup of barley, ground in a food processor or blender

- 1 cup of purified or distilled water

- Breast milk or formula as desired

Bring the water to boil and add in the ground barley. Let simmer for 10 minutes, stirring occasionally. Pour into a bowl and let cool a bit. Mix in milk until you reach the desired consistency.

Really Good Rice Cereal (4-6 months +)

- ¼ cup brown rice ground in food processor or blender

- 1 cup of purified water

Bring the water to a boil in small pan. Stir constantly while adding the rice powder and simmer for about 10 minutes. Transfer to a bowl and allow to cool to lukewarm temperature then add in desired amount of milk.

Oh So Yummy Oatmeal Cereal (4-6 months +)

- ¼ cup oatmeal ground in blender (NOT quick-cook or instant)

- ¾ cup of distilled or purified water

In a small pan, bring the water to a boil. Add in the oatmeal while stirring. Simmer about 10 minutes. Allow to cool until lukewarm then add milk as desired.

Apricot Delight (6 months +)

- ½ pound of apricots, dried

- 1 cup of diluted juice (white grape, apple or pear)

Bring the liquid to a boil in a small saucepan and add in the fruit. Simmer for 10-15 minutes. Place the fruit in a blender or food processor and puree until of smooth consistency. Add the leftover liquids and continue to puree.

Apples to Apples (6 to 8 months+)

- 1 apple

- Distilled or purified water

Peel and core the apple, cutting into slices. Boil until tender. Use a potato masher, blender or food processor to puree the apple.

Banana Apple Bash (4-6 months +)

- 1 banana

- 1 apple

- Distilled or purified water

Peel, core and cut one apple then boil it in a small amount of water until tender. Mash with potato masher or blend in a food processor or blender until smooth. Peel and mash one banana and add to the apple mixture.

Avocado (4-6+)

- 1 ripe avocado

Peel and slice an avocado. Mash.

Bite Into This!

- Some mothers like to spend one day a week making baby's food and the other days enjoying NOT making smashed foods. You can freeze portions in ice cube trays or silicone molds and then transfer to freezer bags or non-BPA freezer storage containers. It's best not to  use a microwave to heat it up as it can destroy vitamins and nutrients, but you can let it thaw in the refrigerator or even warm it on the stove.

- A really fun idea is to video your baby each time she tries a new food. It makes a really cute movie when you combine the videos.

- Another cute idea is to get a photo placemat made of your baby in one of her messiest food poses. She can use it for years to come and it will always be good for a giggle.

Chapter Takeaways

1. Babies are generally ready to start experimenting with grain cereals somewhere between the ages of 4-6 months. She will,

however, let you know if she is ready or not; checking with her pediatrician is recommended.

2. It's best to start baby out on a simple single grain that is well diluted with breast milk or formula and distilled and/or purified water.

3. Introduce one new food at a time and wait one week before trying a new one so you can check for any allergic reactions.

4. Citrus, honey and nuts are not recommended for little ones until your pediatrician gives the go-ahead.

5. Making your own baby food is generally healthier for your baby because it is fresher.

Sleep Solutions

"People who say they sleep like a baby, usually don't have one."

- Author Unknown

We've all heard it said that you don't know a good thing until it's gone. Once baby arrives, the fact is that clearly you will not get enough sleep. Even if you nap when your baby naps (as is advised by many), your sleep cycle will be broken and that's when the trouble all begins. But, it doesn't have to be like that. That's right! Keep reading to find out what all new mothers should know.

First and foremost, sleep isn't just something that's coveted, it's necessary. And it's not just interrupted for a new mother, but most likely for the entire family as well. Imagine baby's mother, father and siblings all walking around like zombies, unable to function properly or deal with even the smallest hiccups in the road. That is the reality for many and it's neither good for baby nor for the rest of the family.

The Science of Sleep

Just as we need to eat, drink and breathe, we have to sleep. Not sleeping is not an option. In order to achieve sleep, our bodies have a powerful switch that flips on that makes us not only tired, but sleepy as well. Eventually, it is so overwhelming that this mechanism cannot and  will not be denied. We fall asleep driving, nursing and in the midst of other very important activities.

The need to sleep is so necessary, the lack of it can become not only uncomfortable but even painful. That is why sleep deprivation interrogations are implemented in war and even in criminal investigations. People have been known to do anything to sleep when the need to do so gets too overwhelming. They've given up their country's deepest secrets and confessed to crimes they've committed and even some that they didn't. It's true. Innocent people have plead guilty to crimes just so that they can be left alone... to sleep.

When we sleep, our bodies repair, rejuvenate and grow. Earlier in the book, we went over the different types of sleep cycles and how important they are. Here are some things you may not be aware happen while you are sleeping.

- **Your brain makes decisions.** The old phrase "let me sleep on it" turns out to hold a lot of truth. Creative writers are often advised to go to sleep thinking about their story or book and that the title for it will come to them with the first thought in the morning. Other decisions come easier after a good night's sleep, too. You may go to sleep considering to put your house on the market and wake up with a clear cut answer. Answers just seem to flow after a night's rest and the reason is that your brain is anything but inactive when you sleep. It is working overtime, actually. The difference is that it is working subconsciously and is reviving at the same time.

- **Memories are consolidated and created.** Did you know that when you are sleeping, your brain is forming new memories? It is and is also compacting older ones. This all happens in both REM and non-REM sleep cycles. The hippocampus is the area of the brain that controls memory and that's where the magic takes place. To deprive the hippocampus of sleep will great upset your memory bank, thus making it very difficult, if not impossible to learn or remember important details.

- **Memory of physical activities are learned and remembered.** Amazingly, while you sleep, your brain is processing physical activities like that new tennis swing you were trying. For a child, it might be learning to jump rope. For a little one, walking may be the activity at hand.

- **Your brain renews creativity.** You simply can't be very creative when you are sleepy. Studies show that you are 33% more likely to be creative when you have gotten a good night's sleep.

- **Toxins are cleared while you sleep.** While you sleep, your brain is busy doing a little housecleaning. It clears out such things as neuro-degenerating molecules that are culprits in diseases like Parkinson's and Alzheimer's. Now that's worth sleeping!

This is Your Brain on NO Sleep

The study of sleep dates as far back as 1896. The subject of sleep and the lack of it has fascinated man for centuries and is now such a common subject that there are sleep centers and countless experiments done daily (or nightly).

Functional Magnetic Resonance Imaging (fMRI) has revealed that the lack of sleep reduces blood flow to the brain and reduces metabolism that is linked to healthy cognitive functions. It also confirms that decision making, intelligence, memory, cognitive speed, attention, arousal and general well-being are impaired when sleep is deprived.

Help with Sleep

If you are having trouble sleeping even when your baby is asleep, you certainly do not want to take prescription or over-the-counter sleep aids because you might sleep too well and not wake up when your baby does. But, there are some other things you can do in the alternative therapy realm.

- **Music therapy**. Music therapy is using music to help lull yourself to sleep. It may not be your favorite music that calms you the best so it's a good idea to experiment with different types of music like classical and instrumental, even if your preference is rock.

- **Sleep promoting teas**. Sipping on a high-quality, organic, non-caffeinated tea just before bedtime is relaxing and should help you fall asleep faster. Chamomile is one that is used to calm and relax.

- **Essential oils**. Many people use essential oils to relax and get a good night's sleep. Chamomile, lavender and ylang ylang are among the most popular for the cause. You can run a mister filled with essential oil or you can even rub it on you, like on the bottom of your feet. Taking a soak bath with an essential oil mixed with a carrier oil like olive oil is extremely relaxing.

Baby's Sleep

Your baby has the need to sleep just as you do. Generally, she will make sure she gets hers but not always. Some babies are fretful sleepers. They fight their sleep. Others suffer from such conditions as colic and simply can't sleep.

Before getting into sleep solutions for your little one, it's important to be sure your baby's sleep is safe. This means taking safety precautions to ensure the cradle or crib is in properly baby-proofed.

Safety Check:

- Crib slats should be no further apart than 2 3/8 inches which is about the size of a can of soda. This prevents your baby getting her head and/or body stuck between the bars.

- If you have an older crib, be sure the paint is not peeling or chipping and that it is not lead-based.

- Be certain that the mattress fits snugly and that you cannot fit more than two fingers between the side of the crib and the mattress.

- Drop-side cribs are discouraged for safety reasons.

- Be sure there are no loose items in the crib such as pillows, blankets, sheets, stuffed animals or bumper pads.

- Baby monitors can have loose cords or parts that can pose a hazard if they are within reach of the crib.

- Corner posts can be a risk and should be no higher than 1/16 of an inch and if your crib has a canopy, no shorter than 1/16 of an inch.

- Headboards and footboards with decorative cutouts are not a good idea as your baby could get trapped in the open space.

- Be sure there are no rough places in the wood that could present splinters.

- Always check your baby's clothing to be sure there is not so much excess that her breathing could be hampered.

NOTE: Electronics and lights rob baby of quality sleep. A nightlight inside the baby's room is questionable so use your own judgment on that and on a baby monitor, air filtration system, vaporizer and so forth — but the less electrical and light in the room, the better.

Understanding Your Baby's Sleep Cycle

Just as older children and adults need sleep, your baby requires adequate sleep, too. Babies sleep determines how well they develop physically, mentally and emotionally.

Your baby's sleep states and sleep cycles are different from your own. Older children and adults have a series of sleep stages including deep and REM sleep. Your baby has two states: active sleep and quiet sleep. These sleep cycles are short, lasting only 50-60 minutes for the initial nine months of her life.

Active sleep is the first stage. It is quite a bit like adult REM sleep, where they can be awakened easily. Fluttering eyelids, some body movements and little noises are characteristic of this mode.

Passive sleep is a deeper sleep. Your baby is less likely to be awakened during this sleep mode, which occurs about halfway through her sleep cycle of 60-90 minutes. Once this cycle completes, your baby either enters the cycle again or she wakes.

How long should a baby sleep?

Your baby's sleep patterns will change with each stage of her life and can be affected by many factors. The chart below will give you a good idea of what to expect given normal circumstances.

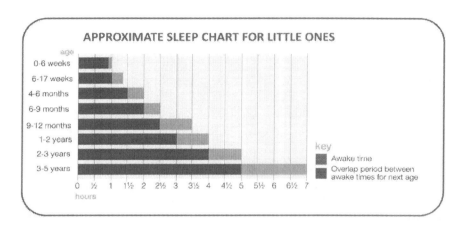

Teach your baby to sleep

Yes, you read it right. You CAN teach your little one to sleep. But, before doing so, you must first make sure that she is healthy and has no physical ailments disrupting her sleep, she weighs enough to go without eating through the night (5 months of age and 15 pounds is the norm) and that she has not just undergone a major change or milestone. You will also want to make sure that your schedule and the schedule of any additional caregivers allow for the time allotments this will entail.

Know that you aren't alone in worrying about your baby's sleep patterns. In the same study from the UK that earlier mentioned 55 percent of women miss their pre-baby social lives, a highly noted item was that new moms don't feel that they can help teach babies to sleep on a schedule — that the moms themselves are "run about" by what the baby wants to do and when.

Sleeping Chart

It's a good idea to keep a chart of your baby's sleeping habits. That way you can track progress, make notes of things that may be influencing her sleep and also be able to see how her sleep is changing with age.

Sleeping Plan

There are some things you can do to encourage your baby to sleep. Listed below are a few:

- Give her a relaxing bath just before bedtime.

- Read or tell her a story.

- Establish a routine.

- Make pajama time fun.

- Give her a stuffed animal or blanket to signal bedtime.

- Rock her. (It's ok!)

- Sing to her.

Soothe her with bedtime-friendly lotion.

There is also another way to help your baby sleep when her waking up is due to the fact that she wants to eat. To do this, you will go by a strict schedule and slowly wean her down from how much milk she is taking.

Night 1: 8:00- Bedtime

10:30- Feed 8 minutes (4 ounces)

2:30- Feed 8 minutes (4 ounces)

7:00- Wake Up

Night 2: 8:00- Bedtime

10:30- Feed 6 minutes (3 ounces)

2:30- Feed 6 minutes (3 ounces)

7:00- Wake Up

Night 3: 8:00- Bedtime

10:30- Feed 4 minutes (2 ounces)

2:30- Feed 4 minutes (2 ounces)

7:00- Wake Up

Night 4: 8:00- Bedtime

10:30- Feed 2 minutes (1 ounce)

2:30- Feed 2 minutes (1 ounce)

7:00- Wake Up

Night 5: 8:00- Bedtime

7:00- Wake Up

You will want to adjust your schedule according to your baby's schedule before you start. If she is not waking for a 2:30 feeding, certainly don't wake her up for one. If she's eating much more than what the chart states, you won't want her to be really hungry. The chart will give you a basic idea of how to help her wean off the breast or bottle for a good night's sleep.

Sleep Solutions for You and the Family

Getting sleep is a must to function properly and being a good and attentive mother requires you to function properly. You can't be on top of things if you are not alert and you cannot make good decisions concerning yourself and your family if you are not thinking straight. Your entire family needs adequate sleep. So…what can be done?

Here are some suggestions to help you and your family catch more zzz's:

- **Naps**. As often as you can, nap. If you can get the rest of your family to do so as well, that is wonderful. Even a short power nap is helpful.

- **Lay down.** Even if you aren't falling asleep or feel you have a million things to do (and chances are you do), just get off your feet. If your baby is sleeping, you can just rest. Sleep is more likely to come if you are laying down and if nothing else, rest is the next best thing to sleep. The same is true for baby's dad and older siblings. Encourage them to lay down, even if it's while watching a movie.

- **Enlist help with feedings.** Late night and early morning feedings are the cause for much of your sleep deprivation. By getting your spouse or visiting grandparent to take over a shift, it will help you get some sleep.

- **Consider "rooming in."** If you keep your baby's bassinet in your room, you'll spend less time going back and forth for nighttime feedings.

- **Wind down without electronics.** When you are in the transition between wake and sleep, consider a book or writing in a journal rather than catching up on Facebook or emails. Electronics tend to steal energy and are not conducive sleep inducers.

- **De-stress.** A nice bubble bath, a good book or soothing music can help you to ditch your stress and anxiety so you can settle into sleep.

Sleep Points to Ponder

- It is best to put your baby to bed while awake. This helps her get used to going to sleep on her own and some babies wake up scared if they are not in the same place they went to sleep.

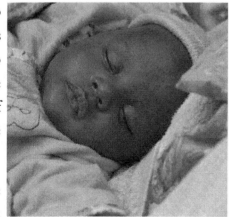

- If your baby sleeps past the set wake-up time, it is a

good idea to wake her unless she is sick. It will help keep her on schedule.

- Your attitude about bedtime will flow over to your baby so keep relaxed about it all.

- If she awakes at night, don't hold her unless you are in the midst of the weaning routine unless of course she is a very young infant who is not ready to wean from late night and early morning feedings. If need be, pat her but try not to do anything at all.

You should begin to see a big change in your entire family once your baby gets the hang of sleeping. Sweet dreams to all!

Chapter Takeaways

1. Sleep is a requirement, not a luxury. Humans cannot function without adequate sleep.

2. Your brain does some marvelous things while you are sleeping like processing information and memories.

3. If you can't nap when baby naps, try just lying down to rest. Encourage your other family members to do so as well.

4. Be you're your baby's sleeping spot is a safe one.

5. By keeping a sleeping chart, you can learn many helpful things about your baby's sleep patterns. But don't get so focused on the chart or measurements that you miss what works for your baby.

The Power of Play

"Life must be lived as PLAY."

- Plato

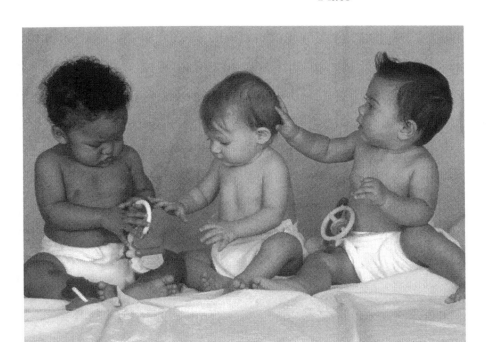

Play is serious business. Even Fred Rogers from Mr. Roger's Neighborhood said so himself. "Play is often talked about as if it were a relief from serious learning. But for children, play is serious learning. Play is really the work of childhood," he said.

How to Play

In the book, "Think Like a Baby" by Amber and Andy Ankowski, it is suggested that you help your baby learn to play from a very young age. Not only does it keep her from getting bored, it stimulates her brain to learn. A rattle or small (safe) toy is enough to do the trick. Now, add some facial expressions and some sounds of your own and you are there… watch your baby begin to follow your lead.

It may sound like a simple task, playing with your little one. And fun, too! But life can get so hectic and stressful, it actually may be an effort at first to unwind and play. You (and she) will be better for it though so go ahead and indulge.

Why Play?

Playing is necessary for babies to properly develop. It is important cognitively, physically, emotionally and socially. Play is how your little one will learn about many things including himself and others as  well as the world around him.

During the first year of your baby's life, everything is new. Just imagine if everything was brand new to you. Think of touching a bright toy, a noisy rattler, a crisp piece of paper all for the very first time. Put yourself in your babe's place and see the world with the wonder that she does. You'll be as excited as she is when you introduce her to play.

Play becomes more imaginative as your child grows. When she is a little older, she will begin to play with others. First it will be playing alongside others and then she will begin to interact. But, first things first. Don't rush her stages for each and every one of them has a very important purpose.

Here are some tips to keep the joy in playing:

- Make it fun and stress-free.

- Don't worry about messes for now. There will be plenty of time to teach her to tidy her messes later when she is older.

Don't stress because your house will look like a zoo of toys. Just go with it and you'll do well.

Dexterity and coordination are learned from playing. Cause and effect are learned as well. Feeling, smelling and even tasting come have a role when your baby is playing. Emotions are explored too. Something is funny and your baby laughs. She is exploring her emotions. Play is a wonderful thing so do all you can to encourage it.

When to Play

Play should be done at appropriate times and that is most of the time except for mealtime and bedtime. Those are events that can be interrupted if your baby associates them with play. Of course there will be food play. That's just part of being a baby and toddler. But don't encourage her to distract from eating and if she has a tendency to do so, you can help get her back on a more serious note. Other than that, anything goes.

For instance, getting dressed can become a game of Peek-a-Boo. Bath time is even better while floating a rubber ducky. Trips in the car are never as long and boring if you are hard at play. Play is great anytime it doesn't get in the way of sleeping or eating.

Play Stages

Birth to One Month

What fun… your baby can now see colors. She loves high contrast. Her vision is now up to an arm's distance. She will grasp and clench at anything so take the opportunity to turn the Palmar Grasp Reflex into a game. She also listens to familiar voices so incorporate some noise into the games, too. Toys that are easy to grasp will be her favorite at this age. She can also have fun with interaction of familiar people.

Two Months

Your baby is now ready for some tummy time so why not make a game of it? You will need to make sure she is totally supervised but place her on her tummy and lay a bright colored  toy down. Watch her watch it. You can also play "smiles". Smile at her and she'll smile back. Bright colored rattles and toys she can grasp as well as plush stuffed animals or dolls.

Three Months

Now it's time for some brain games. Reading brightly colored picture books to her makes a fun game if you animate the characters. You can also start the game of "peek-a-boo" (a favorite of all kids). Baby books (especially the wipe-able, chewable kind), learning interactive toys and ones that she can easily clutch are perfect to introduce at this age.

Four to Six Months

Hand-eye coordination is the name of the game now. Play games where you hold an object out for her to grab. If she grabs onto it, she wins! She will love actually interacting with you and others. Stuffed toys, toys that are easy to clutch and exercise gyms are perfect toys for this age.

Six to Nine Months

Six to nine months of age is a time of exploration. Baby's hand-eye coordination will be developing much more, too. Stackable toys are great at this age as well as crawl balls that encourage her to get around. Cloth and wipe-able books that he can carry are good. Stuffed animals and baby dolls are excellent at this age but beware, she may get attached to one or more of them so you'd better help her keep up with them or get a back-up for "just in case".

Nine to Twelve Months

Your baby is now raring to achieve. She likes to stack, sort and put things in things. What a fun age! You can play games like easy hide-and-go-seek with toys and take turns stacking,  sorting or whatever it is she is into. Toys that move are good, too, as baby is going mobile.

Toys that move when she hits a button, stacking blocks, sorting toys, books, shape sorters and activity centers are awesome toys for this fun age.

Playful Tips

- Get down on the floor and play *with* your little one.

- Play what she wants to play.

- Introduce play when your baby is rested and feels playful.

- Make playing a time to introduce new things.

- Never assume a toy is safe until you have checked it out.

- When she's had enough, it's time to stop.

108

There's nothing more fun than watching a two year-old play. Because she is getting so good at so many things, she's now able to have a blast playing. Her imagination is budding,  which makes her all the more fun. If you are ever having a bad day, just take some time to watch your little one play and you'll feel better in no time.

Skills for Thrills with Toddlers

Busy, busy, busy. Your child will spend much of her day playing at this age. Here are some of the ways your little enjoys her playtime.

- Is interested in others, watches and makes eye contact with them

- Turns her head when she hears her name called

- Engages in some social situations

- Points to things and people

- Can play in small groups

- Can locate things you point to

- Enjoys musical toys

- Likes to listen and look at books

- Loves to pretend

- Enjoys being swung

- Likes being gently thrown into the air

- Explores the playground with glee

- Likes new fun environments

- Likes new toys for experimenting

- Plays with toys without mouthing on them

- Loves new textures

Recommended Play Time

Two year-olds can hardly sit still for any given amount of time. They have to be busy and play. As it turns out, your baby is right on cue with her passion for playing.

Experts recommend that for children between the ages of 12-36 months, 30 minutes per day of their play should be structured by an adult. At least one hour should be free play. It is also advised that your little not be still for over one hour at a time unless she is asleep.

Playmates

Especially as your two year-old reaches the end of the year, she will begin to really show an interest in playing with other children. While she may have played with older siblings all along, the social skills required to interact with those her own age are much more advanced. She'll be working on learning to put the needs and desires of her peers ahead of her own which is a huge feat and often falls under the category of sharing. For now, she is busy observing those her age and probably enjoys playing next to them.

Head to Head

Your little one is advancing so much in the way in which she plays. It used to be all about touching, looking and listening. But now, she is focused on learning. She can solve some problems like which shape goes in which slot and does a good bit of trial-and-error problems solving in her head before physically trying it out.

The cognitive abilities of your little one is working are nothing short of amazing. Her memory is getting sharp and she is understanding concepts - like the fact that she can play with another toy after she picks up the last one she had in her hands.

Fantasy and make-believe are becoming big at this age. Although she still has a little trouble telling them apart, she will love to pretend. When she plays like she is a princess, to some extent, she *is* a princess.

When you are helping your child count out toys, she will begin to *get* the concept of counting and the reason for counting. When you divvy out snacks or toys, she sees that two is better than one in the case at hand. She will most likely LOVE the number two, by the way.

You will also see that your little one alternates play and overlaps activities. She may put a doll to sleep and then go play blocks. She will stop playing blocks to go feed the baby doll.

Play is becoming more complex because your little one is becoming more complex. It is fun to watch how her playtime advances from one day to the next and from month-to-month. Her play will not only entertain her, it will entertain you as well.

Let the Games Begin

The more you actually play with your baby, the better. It is good for both of you. You'll be bonded and refreshed after a round or two of these fun games.

- Follow the leader

- "Ring Around the Rosy"

- Charades, baby style

- Play ball

- Build with blocks

- Imagination games

- Dress up games

Play it Forward

Your baby is using her skills while she is engaging in play and acquiring new ones as she does so. In addition to learning and using and acquiring new skills, play also reduces stress. It is designed to give your baby's brain good foundation on which to build.

Chapter Takeaways

1. Play is necessary for your baby's development. Your little one loves to play and can do many new things.

2. Babies learn and grow intellectually, socially, physically and emotionally while at play.

3. Babies play alone first and then alongside others and then with others. New skills make playing much more fun at this age.

4. Your little one should engage in 30 minutes of structured play per day. However, at least one hour per day should be devoted to unstructured play.

5. Your little will begin to show interest in playing with others his age at the beginning of this year.

Sooo Big: Growth and Development

"Children are not things to be molded, but are people to be unfolded."

\- Jess Lair

You are going to be completely amazed at how your little one grows in just twelve short months. It is astounding to watch. She will go from a helpless little newborn that pees, poops, eats and cries to an active little human.

As your baby grows physically, she will be growing emotionally and intellectually as well. Every part of her will be changing and maturing. This chapter is dedicated to giving a rough calculation on some milestones that will most likely take place and is to be used as an estimated gage. Every child is different. While one child might talk very early and crawl and walk late, the next may do the opposite. It's important not to get all worried and worked up if your child is running behind on any one thing. It is wise, however, to check with her pediatrician if you are concerned.

Baby Power

As your baby grows there's an ignition swit control it all. The brain power source for how baby learns, how much learns, how well sl learns, how she grows  and how well she develops. It is the key to life.

There are some things that will greatly influence her brain and the ability for her to use it to its potential. In Dr. Medina's book, those five things are:

1. The desire to explore.

2. The ability to exercise self-control.

3. The desire and ability to practice creativity.

4. The ability to communicate.

5. The ability to interpret non-verbal communication.

It is within the realms of these five factors that your baby will be able to properly build upon that which was bestowed on her through DNA and happenstance intelligence which is how she is wired, some of us being naturally smarter than others with no explanation.

While some things you cannot control in her brain development, there are a ton of things that you do have so much control over it will leave you nervously in awe. Parenting is a huge responsibility. As a parent, you have the ability to make or break that which your baby becomes, the way in which her brain blossoms or withers.

Seed

Brain seeds are sown while your baby is in your womb and even before. Your DNA, your nutrition, your activities, your attitude and many other factors contribute to your baby's brain development.

Soil

The setting and atmosphere you create for your baby to learn within is like the soil in which you would grow a flower. If you fertilize it with praise, positivity and set her up to succeed, chances are that she will. On the other hand, if you don't do much or anything and show no interest or, you push her too hard, criticize her and make her feel as if she is inadequate, you will fill the soil with toxins and she will not flourish.

Here are some ways to help ensure that your baby's brain is nurtured:

- **Be sure to make her feels safe.** A brain cannot learn if it does not feel safe.

- **Breast feed for a year.** Studies prove that the mother's brain sends the necessary nutrients, custom-made, for ultimate brain development.

- **Talk to your baby.** Talking and being talked to increases IQ.

- **Read to your baby.** Babies who have books to them make better readers.

- **Praise effort rather than result.** Teach her that giving it her all is the key.

When it comes to your baby's brain, think of yourself as a gardener. What you sow, you reap. Be sure that you are doing all you can to ensure a blossoming, beautiful brain.

Sight

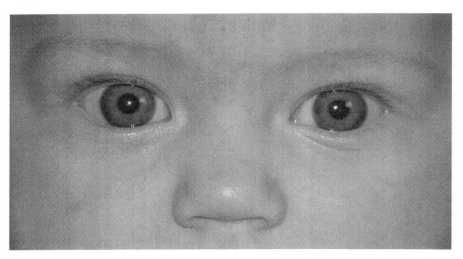

Your baby's sight will change dramatically during the first year. It's important to know what is normal and what abnormalities to keep a watch out for. Here's a little insight on your little one's sight:

- **Newborn.** Things are a bit fuzzy at this age. She will turn to the light, however, and blink in response to a sudden or bright light source. She will often fixate on an object of interest. Her sight range is about 7-10 inches and that means if you are holding her, you should be in her view.

- **One month.** She can see your face clearly when you are holding her. She will begin to study your features. Although she can now see in color, she's not yet able to tell the difference. Black and white and highly-contrasted colors are appealing to her.

- **Two months.** Now she is beginning to see a difference in colors. She can distinguish between shapes and is probably really liking bright, primary colors. This is a great time to introduce brightly colored toys and books.

- **Four months.** Your little one is beginning to be able to tell distance. She has depth perception. She will begin to grab for things like toys as well as your hair and jewelry.

- **Five months.** Things are getting fun. She is examining things closely and can spot something at a distance. You can play "where is the…" with her and she'll point or look in the direction of the object or… in the direction of where you hid it. Another fun game is "copycat" because as she is starting to mimic, it's hilarious.

- **Eight months.** Your little one is seeing life more clearly now. She almost has the vision of an adult. She recognizes people and even objects from all the way across the room.

- **Nine months.** If you've been wondering what color your baby's eyes are going to be, you probably have your answer. Chances are they will stay the same color as they are in her ninth month. Her vision is getting sharper; she may point to an object and want it.

- **Twelve months.** Along with recognizing people and objects from afar, your babe can tell the distance between something near and far.

Eye-Opening Tips

- Eye tests for children under 16 years of age are free.

- Her doctor will most likely check her eyes between six and eight months of age.

- Be sure to have her eyes checked when her pediatrician recommends it.

- Report any problems, such as crossed eyes or a lazy eye.

- Excessive squinting should be acknowledged.

- Wandering eyes should be mentioned.

- Low birth weight babies sometimes have a condition call retinopathy where oxygen fills with the blood within the eye.

There is a very successful treatment so don't fret but do have it seen about.

Hearing

A baby's hearing is amazingly good, even in the womb. You may have noticed her response to loud noises while she was in your tummy and you most likely see her react now that she is born.

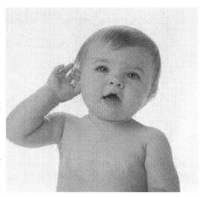

By the age of six months, your little one's hearing will be caught up to that of an adult.

Hear (pun intended) is what you can expect in the first year:

- **Newborn.** At birth, your babe's ears are still full of fluid that will clear in time. The parts of her brain that cause her to hear are still developing so although she can hear, she doesn't hear as good as she will.

- **Three months.** Your baby will begin to really pay attention to sounds, especially those that are high in pitch. She will also show interest in familiar noises such as your voice.

- **Four months.** This is a really fun age when you get to see your baby get excited when she hears a familiar sound. She may also start to mimic sounds that she hears.

- **Six months.** Ahhh... a cute milestone takes place at this age. Your little one is becoming aware of where sounds actually originate. After hearing a noise, she will often turn towards it. Quiet noises are of interest to her as well.

- **Twelve months.** By one year of age, your little one can most likely recognize her favorite songs and may even try to join in singing them.

Here are some tips to help teach your little one to listen:

- Sing nursery rhymes and play music.

- Make lots of different sounds.

- Read to your baby.

- Change the pitch of your voice often.

Some ways you can tell if your baby has hearing problems are:

- She never waking to loud sounds.

- She doesn't turn or startle to loud sounds as she gets older.

- She pulls on her ear.

- A hearing test is done at birth but you can request another one later.

Smelling

Did you know that your baby's sense of smell is most powerful at birth? Smell is actually processed by the same part of the brain that controls memory and research proves that your baby could  even smell in the womb. Fascinating!

For the first few months, she will favor your scent above anyone else's. That is most likely because she is, by now, so used to it. One has to wonder how that plays into the brains will to survive and how it is programmed to do things that encourage survival. Even young animals in the wild find their mothers by sense of smell.

As your little one's first year ends, she will begin to explore her sense of smell. She will start to show favored smells. Some smells will invigorate her while others will sooth her. It is fun to learn which does what.

Here are some ways to enhance your baby's sense of smell.

- Let her smell a flower.

- Let her smell baking bread.

- Let her smell leather.

- Let her smell an essential oil.

Tasting

You baby began her tasting when in the womb, around seven weeks in utero, to be exact. Many pregnant mothers do not realize how true it is that they are eating for two. She has had a buffet by the time she is born.

Newborns. Most babies are born with a sweet tooth. Did you know that both breast milk and formula are sweet? Most newborns are not fans of bitter or sour tastes, not that it's a good idea to offer those to her.

Four months. Your little one might just get a knack for salty tastes during this time. Believe it or not, the taste of your breast milk is changing wildly. One day it might taste of garlic and the next day of mint. This is preparing your little one for a smorgasbord of flavors.

Tips to Tempt the Taste Buds:

- Let baby see you eat a good variety of foods.

- Make "mmm" noises as you eat different foods.

- When your little one is old enough, introduce him to foods in a very positive and fun manner.

- Introducing spicy foods should be done slowly or they may leave a bad taste in her mouth for future efforts.

- Remember that things you eat affect the flavors of your milk, so be mindful of too many complex flavors at once for your little one.

Touching

Your baby's sense of touch is more important than you may realize. Babies can be calmed through baby massage therapy and learn through touch as well. Touch relays many messages within the brain such as communication of emotions. Your baby's sense of touch began about  eight weeks into your pregnancy and will be developing rapidly throughout her first year.

- **Newborn.** Your baby's mouth, cheeks, face and hands are extra sensitive to his touch. Even the soles of her feet relay a burst of feelings. She will respond to your touch with a grasp of her little hand.

- **One month.** At this age, your baby will have her hands grasped shut much of the time but when open, she will love clutching on to your finger when you tickle or touch her palm.

- **Two to three months.** If you are in tune with your little one, you will note that she loves you to touch her.

- **Four months.** Her muscles are growing stronger and she will now start to reach out and touch objects and people, too.

- **Five months.** Although she is reaching for things and sometimes even securing them, much of her sense of touch is done by way of her mouth.

- **Six months.** Interaction toys are excellent at this age because your little one is all about touching and exploring.

- **Seven to eight months.** The wonderful world of 3D touch is being discovered.

- **Nine months.** Your mobile baby is touching everything so it's a good time to double check things are touchable (such as ovens, fireplaces, et cetera).

- **One year.** Hard, soft, cold, warm, wet, squishy, sticky… all of the senses are being explored as baby's sense of touch matures.

Baby Massage

- Stroking, caressing and tickling will often calm your baby.

- Kangaroo Care is a method used that entails carrying your baby close to your bare chest for skin-to-skin touch that calms and quietens and is also proven to increase her oxygen levels.

- Regular massage brings about bonding as well as comfort.

Reflexes

Once again, the brain displays its primitive will to survive, this time through the manifestation of reflexes.

Here are some newborn reflexes that exhibit touch:

- Sucking reflex (where your baby sucks on anything put in his mouth).

- Rooting (when a baby sucks due to her mouth being stroked).

- Moro reflex (when your baby feels like he is falling).

- Grasp reflex (when your baby grasps everything he can).

- Babinski reflex (when his big toe extends out even when the other toes aren't).

- Tonic neck reflex (when your baby turns his neck and extends his arm out, usually when laying on his back).

- Step reflex (when your little one takes a step when he feels his foot touch something such as the floor).

These primitive newborn reflexes give way to adult reflexes when a baby is healthy. In situations where there is a disease or neurological defect, the reflexes tend to linger, most likely the body and brain's way of defending life.

First Year Milestones

Below are some milestone markers to use as a roundabout gage for judging your baby's growth and development. If you have concerns, don't stress. Talk to her pediatrician and go from there. It is normal for babies to excel in one area and lag in another.

One Month

- Loves human shapes and prefers them to other shapes

- Lifts head for short intervals

- Moves head to one side and then the other

- Arms make jerky movements

- Focuses on things and people 8-12 inches away

- Turns to familiar sounds (maybe)

- Blinks at lights when they are bright

- Strong reflex movements

- Responds to sounds that are loud

End of Second Month

- Tracks objects and people with her eyes

- Smiles

- Begins to make noises

- Begins to make vowels sounds (maybe)

End of Third Month

- Lifts head at a 45 degree angle

- Raises chest and head when in tummy time

- When on her back, kicks and straightens her legs

- Opens and closes her little hands

- Can track objects that are in motion

- Imitates sounds (maybe)

- Reaches for objects that are dangling

- When on a hard surface, she pushes down with her legs

- Shakes and grasps rattles and hand toys

- Brings hands together

- Recognizes familiar faces and objects

- Develops a social smile

- Is getting a grip on hand-eye coordination

- Kicks with vigor

- Is developing control of holding her head up

By the End of Fourth Month

- May sleep a total of six hours per night without waking (yay!)

- Typically sleeps 15-17 hours a day total

- Rolls from stomach to back (and possibly back to tummy)

- Lifts head up at 90 degree angle

- Is beginning to sit with support

- Follows objects and people at a 180-degree arc

- Entertains herself with babble

- Is responsive to colors and even shades

- Recognizes items such as her bottle

- Explores many things with her mouth

- Is getting pro at communicating things like discomfort and happiness

- Is responsive to noises

By the End of Month Five

- Is beginning to spy things across the room

- Is attentive to small objects

- May begin to experiment with cause and effect

- Rakes toys closer

- May begin teething

By the End of Month Six

- Reaches out and grabs things

- Opens mouth for a bite

- Sits with little support

- Has good head control when being pulled to sitting position

- Rolls over and then back

- Can drink from a cup with a little help

- Is able to hold her bottle

- Mimics some facial expressions

- Is beginning to make two-syllable sounds

By the End of Month Seven

- Can tell the difference in voice tones

- Is able to feed herself some finger foods

- Makes sounds of wet razzing

- When talked to, turns in direction of the voice

- Begins to imitate

- Plays peek-a-boo

- Can distinguish emotions in tone of voices

By the End of Month Eight

- Loves to chew on objects

- Reaches for spoon when being fed

- Sleeps around 11-13 hours per night

- Takes 2 or 3 naps

- Rolls all the way over

- Can sit unsupported

- Babbles

- Has certain cries for certain things

- Doesn't like to be removed from Mommy or a specific person

- Responds to her name

- Likes to drop things intentionally

- Feeds herself many finger foods

By the End of Month Nine

- Reaches for her toys and other items

- Looks for things after dropping them

- Can go from her tummy to sitting alone

- Picks up very tiny things (good time to vacuum)

- Can recognize herself in a mirror

By the End of Month Ten

- Pulls to a standing position

- Doesn't like a toy to be removed

- Is able to transfer things from one hand to the other

- Stands holding on to something or someone

By the End of Month Eleven

- Says a few simple words like "ma-ma" or "da-da"

- Gets the meaning of the word "no"

- Waves bye-bye

- Claps her hands

By the End of Month Twelve

- Has most likely tripled her birth weight

- Takes one to two naps per day

- Loves to bang objects together

- Crawls

- Cruises

- Enjoys opening and closing cabinet doors (good time to double check baby proofing)

- Shakes her little head "no"

- May voluntarily let a toy or object go

- Loves to put things into containers

- Walks with help

- Dances

- Shares (somewhat)

- May be afraid of strangers

- Shows interest in books

- Understands simple commands

- May become attached to something like a toy or blanket

- Likes to pull, push and dump things

- Is beginning to understand what some things are called

- Tests responses of her behavior

- Tries to help when getting dressed

- Pulls hat and socks off

- Knows who she is in a mirror

What will change when your baby becomes a toddler? Everything. The world is so full of wonder, it's often difficult to keep a handle on him. You may find yourself doing some things you thought you'd never do. Remember how you used to gawk at mothers who opened snacks in the grocery store just to shut their screaming kid up? I believe the name for it is "grazing" and it is, in some stores, considered shoplifting. Well, not only do you now sympathize with grazers, you also have been known to promptly exit the store once your little one has thrown the goodies in a random rage. "Clean up on aisle four," you hear across the speaker as you leave. You just keep walking.

Toddler Transitions

If you have never experienced being around a toddler, you are in for a real treat. It is suggested that spending the day caring for a one year-old is a great form of birth control.

Yes, they are *that* difficult... sometimes. But, other times, they are definition of delight. A toddler is a mini-mix of all that is terrific and all that is terrible, all rolled up into one adorable package.

Your little "one" will be so busy exploring, physically and emotionally, it will make your head spin. You will be exhausted to say the least. Be sure and refer back to the suggestions for de-stressing and also the helpful information on your love-life relationship... you will need those tools.

One thing is for certain, you will want to have a camera handy, so have your cell phone ready. Your one year-old will be doing new things all the time. Some things will leave your horrified and others will leave you so proud you can't stand it. Your baby is growing up; enjoy the journey. It only happens once.

Toddler Basics

See how absolutely adorable the little guy is in the photo to the right? That's a typical toddler for you. He's so cute you just want to watch him all day long and...you'd better. Do you also see the flowers he is beholding? They are poisonous if ingested.

Toddlers are busy. You will be, too. You've got to keep up with them or they can get into very real trouble.

Your little one has most likely become very mobile. If she isn't walking yet, she is probably crawling like crazy and cruising, too.

Not only is she very active physically, her brain is quite busy as well. During the twelfth to twenty-fourth month, many developments will occur on all levels.

Learning

You can blame much of her typical toddler behavior on her overwhelming desire to learn. It gets the best of her. By touching, smelling, tasting and trying everything, she is learning by leaps and bounds.

She is most likely:

- Walking or attempting to walk.

- Dancing.

- Communicating.

- Sliding. Squeezing, pushing and pulling objects.

- Climbing steps, one at a time.

- Holding a crayon.

- Focusing on objects both near and far.

- Throwing things.

- Retrieving things.

Social Skills

Although her social skills have come so far since the day she came into this world, it is often obvious how immature they are. It is in her attempt to further her social skills that 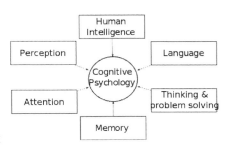 many of the tell-tale toddler characteristics become evident. She will experience emotions in epic proportions. On a scale of 1-10, hers will many times be 1,000.

Here are some facts about the average one year-old.

- May be afraid of strangers

- Can become anxious or shy at the drop of a hat

- Imitates those around her

- Tests the limits of you and other caregivers

- Claims everything she likes as "mine"

- Is temperamental

- Is developing a keen sense of self

- Is very egocentric

- Realizes she is separate from you and others

- Gets angry, proud and scared

- Likes to choose

- Is becoming more independent

Cognitive Development

Just behind your little one's forehead sits a part of her brain called the frontal lobe. Together with the temporal lobes, cognitive skills are formed through specific neuronal networks.

Cognitive skills and abilities are core skills that her brain uses in order to do such things as learn, remember, reason, think, read (later on) and pay attention. Cognitive skills will allow her to take incoming information and move it to its correct place into the place where knowledge is stored. These skills are necessary in order to thrive at school, play, work (later on) and in life.

Here are some ways that she is growing cognitively.

- Can follow simple instructions

- Sees cause and effect

- Has the desire to experiment

- Wants to explore

- Loves repetition

- Asks questions

- Imitates others

- Plays with sounds

- Is developing her vocabulary

Physical Preparedness

Can anything really prepare us for the changes in store with a toddler in the house? Just when you think you have toddler-proofed every possible thing, you'll find another and yet another danger lurking. There are some good guidelines to get you started though and here's a look at some of them.

Crib

- Be certain you don't have a drop side on the crib.

- Be sure the mattress is down far enough she cannot climb out.

- Don't leave toys in the crib he can stack to climb up and out.

Bed

- When your little one is about 35" tall, it's a good idea to move her into a bed or toddler bed.

- A bed with a rail is safest.

- A mattress on the floor is often a good transition from crib to bed.

Beware of Burns

- Be extremely careful of carrying hot liquids such as coffee. Toddlers are always underfoot.

- Don't sit hot food or drinks on coffee tables or edges of tables or counters.

- Keep your child contained when you cook; never hold her and cook.

- Install a guard for the stove and covers for stove knobs.

- Turn pot pans so that they face the back of the stove and can't be grabbed.

- Secure an oven latch on the door.

Doors and Windows

- Doorstops and door holders can help protect little fingers.

- Keep doors locked so she can't wander out them.

- Don't leave her unattended by an open window.

- Don't have her play area right beside a low window.

Electrical Outlets, Appliances and Cords

- Be sure you have outlet covers installed.

- Be sure to have child-safety outlets in place.

- Have cords out of reach.

- Keep blow dryers and other small appliances out of reach.

Falls

- Never leave your child in her highchair unattended or where she can get onto the furniture.

- Secure all stairs and balcony areas with a child gate or locked door.

- Use window guards.

- Don't leave window blind cords loosely hanging.

- Be sure any railings don't have openings wider than 3 ½ inches. If they do, block them.

- Safely buckle her in when using a shopping cart or stroller.

Fireplaces and Wood Burning Stoves

- Install a grill on the front of your fireplace or stove.

- Use a baby fence when the source is in use.

- Teach your little one what "hot" is and enforce the fact the fireplace or stove is hot!

Danger Zones: Off Limits

- Teach your child that swimming pool areas are off limits without you but be sure pools and hot tubs are secured with fences and locked gates.

- Cabinets and pantries should be off-limits but child-proofed anyway.

- Bathrooms should be off-limits but precautions taken "just in case" like locking toilet lids.

Secure

- Secure all shelves to the wall.

- Teach your children not to climb on shelves or furniture but child-proof them as best you can all the same.

- Go back through the baby-proofing suggestions in the first of this book to be sure you are still up to the guidelines.

Emotional Preparedness

What will truly prepare you for your toddler is only your toddler. There's really no way to begin to know what your little one will be like. You may have the perfect angel or not. Even at best, there will be tempers, tantrums, trial and tribulations but there will be triumphs that makes it all worthwhile.

Mending at the Source

Not only are you wondering who you've become, your husband, friends and family are as well. While your toddler is an ornery mess, she's cute as a bug and steals the hearts of all. You, on the other hand, are simply seen as a raving maniac.

It's time to take a little time out. Check out the suggestions below for some tried and true ways to reclaim your sanity:

- Regularly have a day or even half-a-day that you do something you enjoy.

- Go to lunch with a friend and leave your little one with a sitter or your partner..

- Take up Yoga.

- Join an online toddler parent support group.

- Repeat often, "This too shall pass."

- Remember, it's not your fault. Toddlers will be toddlers.

Chapter Takeaways

1. Now that your little one is mobile, it's time to toddler-proof... EVERYWHERE.

2. You will want to go back over the first of this book to take another look at suggestions for keeping the relationship with your spouse healthy.

3. Your toddler is not only go to be physically busy but her brain is very active as well. Milestones are best used as general

guides. Never stress you're your baby's lagging as it is most likely normal.

4. Little ones learn by touching, smelling, tasting, exploring and experimenting. This makes it very important to keep a watchful eye on your toddler at all times.

5. Toddlers will be toddlers. Situations presented by them does not mean you are a bad parent.

Dare to Discipline

"Parenthood... It's about guiding the next generation, and forgiving the last."

- Peter Krause

The way or ways you choose to discipline (or not discipline) your child is your right as a parent, as long as it is within the realms of the law. Most likely you will work alongside your spouse, listen to other parents with well-behaved children (perhaps even your own parents), go with a good bit of your spiritual and moral values and read and listen to good teachings on the subject. Somewhere in the midst, you will incorporate your own system.

There are many philosophies on rearing children. It is certainly worth taking many ideas into account to take what you like and discard the rest. Parenting is a huge responsibility. You are molding a human being. The task deserves the time and trouble involved to research and soul search as well.

Methods

Brazelton

"Discipline: The Brazelton Way" is a book by Berry Brazelton and Joshua Sparrow. It is built around the concept that each and every temper tantrum of act of disobedience is an opportunity to help your child grow. Here are some remedies suggested for various misbehaviors:

- Discipline should be individually tailored to your child.

- By the age of three months, parents should be guiding their baby into a pattern.

- At age seven to eight months, a baby is ready for some boundaries and limits.

- Safety should be taught at an early age... not just implemented but taught.

- By nine months of age, your baby can recognize your non-verbal expressions so take the opportunity to use this as a teaching tool.

- Stand strong when your baby tests you but be patient as this is a normal part of growing up.

- Your commands will need to be repeated and repeated when baby is young.

Age Appropriate Discipline

You certainly don't tell your six month old to take a time out. Neither do you want to allow your two year-old to get by with everything. Here are some stages of growth and understanding that can  help you gage what discipline is appropriate… and what is not.

- **8-12 months.** By this age, your little one very well may be crawling around. Being mobile means the potential for danger (which certainly means, a little discipline will be in order).

One thing to keep in mind is that your baby will react to the word "no" more by the tone of voice you use than by the actual word. Thus, it is not practical to trust that she is going to obey your command each and every time. Therefore, as much as possible, the danger should simply be removed from her path. If your purse is on the coffee table, moving it is a good idea. There are other dangers, however, that cannot simply be removed such as a hot stove. Telling her "no" is, for sure, a good idea but also moving her from the scene is practical as well.

- **12-24 months.** By now, your little one is catching on to the meaning of words. You can tell him "no" and he will know what that means. You can even start to communicate even more such as naming the specific act he is not supposed to do like touching the picture or pulling your hair. He may not understand fully, but is much closer to grasping it all not.

  This is also a good age to begin to explain "why." He probably won't understand half of what you are telling him, but he will get some of it. When he hits, you can tell him that he cannot do so and that…it hurts. Eventually, he'll understand.

- **24-36 months.** As your little one is getting bigger, so are the expectations that must be placed on her. It is imperative to teach her about safety like the stove is hot, traffic is dangerous. Then there will be new things that will come her way, like getting along with other children and appropriate behavior when in public.

  Sharing is a big deal at this age. She will most likely say that everything is hers because, until you teach her otherwise, that is exactly what she believes. Now is the time to let her in on the secret that not everything is hers. If you approach it in a positive manner, like showing her that sharing is nice, you will have much better luck.

  This is also the age that a time out may be in order. It's good to have certain bad behaviors that warrant such punishment like if she intentionally does something she knows is wrong. Keeping a consistency about your discipline measures is really important at this age, too.

Breaking the Will without Breaking the Spirit

Best-selling Christian author and psychologist James Dobson talks about discipline in many of his parenting books, including "The Strong Willed Child." He adamantly defends that children under one year of age are not yet ready for discipline. He does, however, suggest they should be lovingly led and guided, even from the first days of their lives. Learning by example is a big part of his theology.

Some of his methods involve:

- Repetition is a must.

- Structure is imperative.

- Consistency is a must.

- Loving discipline is the name of the game.

- Always make sure your child knows it is her actions, not her, that are not liked.

- Explain what she did wrong, even when very young.

Getting Over It

Television reality talk show host and psychologist, Dr. Phil McGraw, is famous for saying, "Get over it." Sometimes it's what truly has to take place in order to move forward.

No doubt you have some baggage from your past. The manner in which you were disciplined (or not disciplined) was perhaps not optimal. It is imperative that you come to terms with letting go of those memories so you don't subconsciously repeat them. And yes, that does happen more often than not. Choose the things you liked about how you were discipline and incorporate those things into your own and the rest just ditch.

If you find this impossible to do, it's worth seeking the help of a professional. It's not a shame to do so, it's a shame to <u>not</u>. Talk therapy is useful in order to work through issues of your past. Sometimes just vocalizing what you went through as a child makes a huge difference. Your counselor or even a self-help book can guide you down the right path for ditching the old to make room for the new.

On the Same Page

You and your spouse will simply have to be on the same page with discipline. Rarely do two parents totally agree on everything so you will need to work through it by compromising and communication. If need be, consult a professional. If you are divided, you will not be able to root your child in love and consistency when disciplining and you are asking for a can of worms. Together, the two of you can work in unity to raise a wonderful responsible human being.

Tried and True Tips on Discipline

- Newborns simply need to be loved. There generally is no spoiling at this age. They have the desire to be safe and secure and it is up to you to provide for this need.

- Between the fourth and seventh month, your baby will probably begin to pull and tug. This is a good time to begin to teach them "no."

- Around seven to twelve months of age, you can begin to teach your child safety. "Hot" is one to teach; of course, you never let them actually touch something too hot, but rather let them feel the heat to a safe extent.

- When your child becomes mobile, you will begin to implement and reinforce the word "no" by physically moving them from the situation.

- Always reinforce every act of discipline with positivity and love.

Setting the Stage

During their first year, there will be two main stages your child will go through. You may want to take that into consideration when you discipline. Here are the stages and suggestions:

12-18 months

Your little one will be very vocal when you start to discipline her. She will probably object very loudly. Some of her first discipline will probably stem from her tantrums of screaming in public and other bouts of rage. She is going through huge emotional changes and believe it or not, as you decide what is too much, you will be helping her as well as yourself and others.

18-24 months

Some of your child's misbehavior will have to do with what she is learning at this age. No…that's not a ticket out of trouble but it is a reality. She is learning language and may spout off with talking back to you. You may say "no" and she tells YOU  "no." Of course, this is not acceptable but it will be up to you to lovingly teach her that.

Children in this stage get easily frustrated and may break out in a tantrum at any given time. Of course, that is not acceptable either. You will certainly need to give her guidance during this phase of her life or she will be a holy terror. Discipline is for her sake and everyone else's as well.

Safety is a big issue at this age. She'll be into everything and must learn what is off-limits. For sure, it is time to discipline when she is able to get into danger.

By the age of two, your little one is ready to be guided by some discipline. If not, it will surely show. Although there will still be temper tantrums and situations of defiance to handle, you will notice a decrease in the terrible outbursts once you consistently show her who is boss. She has to learn she is not because is pretty sure that she is at this point.

Why are They Called the Terrible Twos?

On a good day, many parents make the comment that the terrible twos are not so terrible after all. However, some of them are parents of three year-olds though and are swearing *that* is the age of monstrosity.

Sometimes, your two year-old will be simply angelic. You will now be able to reason with her to some extent and get some cooperation at times. In many ways, things will be easier.

But, it's when what she wants and what you want conflict that the trouble begins. Two year olds are on a mission to gain independence to a degree. It is a life stage and is for a very great reason. Eventually, she will be on her own and that journey starts now. But, since she's not ready for that yet, you will need to guide her along the pathway. Often times, she will not like that at all.

Characteristics of a Two Year Old

Here are some things you may find to be true about your little one:

- She heavily resists correction.

- Her emotions are extreme.

- She gets an attitude very quickly.

- Things are all about her much of the time.

Some unrealistic ways you may feel are:

- That she is acting out to spite you.

- That her bad behavior makes you a bad mother.

- That this is the way things will always be.

- That it's you against her.

- That you fail on a daily basis.

Things you can do:

- Realize that raising your little is not a test.

- Know that she is being a typical two year-old and nothing is done intentionally towards you.

- This is NOT the way things will always be.

- As long as you are trying, you are anything but a failure.

Getting the Visual

Sometimes it takes stepping back to see clearly see the big picture. You are the artist creating a masterpiece. During the process, it can certainly seem like a daunting task at times. But, there is a calm after the storm and then a rainbow.

When you are having her pick up her toys and she is balking beyond belief as if you have asked her to pick up the toys for every child in the world, try to visualize her cooperating. As you do so, help her with a positive attitude. Rave at her progress and she'll be encouraged. If you are overwhelmed and stressed, you can only imagine how she is as well.

Getting the visual of the immediate task at hand is great but the visual of the overall big picture is even better. See your little one as who she will become later on in life. Picture having lunch with her as *she* rustles to round up her two year old. The day will come sooner than you think.

Age Appropriate Discipline

The trick of getting your two year-old in line is often in lining up yourself. Your mood, your attitude and your self-control will play a huge role so be sure you are taking care of yourself, your relationship and *then* your little one. When done in that order, things will flow much smoother.

Pick your battles

You've heard it said about love relationships but it's true with your youngster, too. Picking your battles, prioritizing the most important disciplinary matters, prevents you spending all day every day getting on to her. Some things can wait until she is older to deal with while a fit thrown in the supermarket cannot.

Make realistic expectations

Perhaps your child has been taught to help pick up her toys at bedtime. But, company is coming and you are in a mad dash to clean the house. "Pick up your toys," you shout from the other room as you race to clean up the sink full of dirty dishes. You little one continues to play. Can you really expect her to pick her toys up without you helping during a time that is normally designated for play? Your lack of planning really doesn't constitute an emergency on her part, in keeping with the adage. You cannot expect her to feel the importance of the moment, in other words. Don't project your troubles onto her. Make realistic expectations and help her to follow through with them.

Triggers

We all have triggers and by now, you are familiar with some things that seem to set your child off. As best you can, steer clear of those things, especially when she is tired or cross. If you know she is apt to have a meltdown when you go shopping, take her shopping on days she is well-rested. Then, you can deal with any misbehavior, but you are less likely to have a two year-old having a complete temper tantrum in the middle of the aisle.

Be consistent. Let your "yes" be "yes" and your "no" be "no"... every time. Clear and simple. That is only fair for your child and for yourself.

Stay calm. When you "lose it," chances are good your little one will, too. If you are feeling angry or frustrated, do your best to calm down before disciplining. Discipline should always be done in a positive and loving manner. Sometimes that requires removing yourself from the situation until you calm down. That is only natural. Moms are only human.

Time Out

Your child is using all she has to test limits at this age. She runs, climbs, throws and language skills are being used, too. When she tells you no, that is a test using her new skills. It is imperative that you nip these acts of defiance in the bud or her entire life will be an uproar of testing you and every other authority member. But, it is important that you do so by breaking the will without breaking her spirit. Her action is unacceptable, not her.

Time out is appropriate for some actions, especially those that can get her hurt. It's a good idea to have a "time out chair" or a certain spot she is to go to. Make sure to communicate what she did and then have her sit for a short time out. Once the time out is over, assure her you love her but that  she cannot continue the behavior. Keep it short and keep it simple. Most of all, keep it loving. After all, that is why we discipline our children because we love them. You know that, now make sure she knows that, too.

Turning the Terrible Twos into Terrific Twos

It's time to turn the tables. Now that you are well-equipped with the knowledge from this book and your own storehouse of information as well, you can have the most treasured and terrific year  ever with your little one. Being two only happens once. One day you will reminisce and miss the things you are experiencing together today. Ask any mother of a child who is now in high school, college or married with children. Your house will be clean... too clean. It will be quiet... too quiet. By putting all your new skills and knowledge to work, you can make it a joyous year and though your nest will one day be empty, your heart will always be full. Make memories and enjoy being the wonderful mother you becoming and know that it is always about progress, not perfection.

The true journey of discipline begins in the time slot between 12 and 24 months. Although authorities on the subject of child discipline disagree on exactly when it should begin, you will know when. One clue will be when your child's behavior is destructive to herself and/or others. That's when it's time.

Journey of Correction

As discussed earlier in this chapter, there are a myriad of discipline theories and methods. Chances are, you will research all and come up with one of your own, tailor made for your unique little one. Hopefully, you and your spouse can reach agreements on the important things and be in one accord because even at this young age, if you don't, she will sense it and will begin to play sides. The same is true for other caregivers like sitters and grandparents. Everyone must pull together in unity for the sake of the child. Consistency matters.

Testing

Your toddler will constantly be testing the waters. That's what she does. She's a little one. It's her job.

Sometimes she truly may not get it. I mean, why can she cross the street with you and not without you? It is during this year that she will begin to put two and two together so it's the perfect timing for her to learn the rules.

It's important to be persistent. If it's "no" one time, it must be "no" every time. She can't be able to get by with something just because you are tired or busy. That's not fair for her.

Personality

As her personality buds, you will begin to get a glimpse into what your journey will be like. Is she easy to guide? Does she aim to please or is she hell bent on rebelling? One thing to remember is that each personality has its pros and cons. Your compliant child may later prove to be difficult when needing to stand up against peer pressure. Your defiant child, once trained, may be a leader. Keeping these things in mind will help you practice discipline with patience because you will need plenty of patience, trust me.

Watch Her Watch You

She may not be listening, but she is watching. Be sure to make the grade. If you tell her not to throw trash on the floor but are guilty of doing it yourself, she will notice. Of course, that still doesn't mean she can; remember, children learn by example.

Temper

The painful reality is that you are going to be tired, sick, hungry, irritated. Not only will your little one be experiencing emotions on a high level, you probably will be as well. It's easy to get frustrated and all too easy to discipline in anger and frustration. You will need to develop some coping skills of your own in order to disciple her with love.

Here are some suggestions:

- Try to get rest when you can. Things always seem worse when you are exhausted.

- Enlist the help of others when you can.

- Remember that she is but a little one and is full of emotions, too.

- Think of the person she is becoming rather than the toddler that she is. When she argues, picture her as an attorney. That may be her personality. You simply need to mold her.

- If you feel your emotions are out of control, talk to someone. There is no shame in doing so, only in NOT doing so.

Just as there was no fool-proof way to prepare for what lie in store with a little one, there is no way to completely know what the future will hold with your two year-old. But, there are some very helpful materials, thoughts and suggestions in this book and with other parents. You will want to drink in every ounce you can.

Tackling the Terrible Twos: Nipping it in the Bud

Remember, you little one has never been two. She will often be as confused and overwhelmed as you are. You'll get through it together and there will be many wonderful memories to share along the way.

Tips for Two

- Don't get too angry, lonely or tired.

- Don't let her get too angry, lonely or tired.

- Gladly accept help when others offer.

- Keep in mind that the ultimate goal is to raise a responsible, loving adult.

Encourage her to learn and stay positive.

Chapter Takeaways

1. Two year-olds can by trying. It helps to take time out to look at the big picture and remember that having an unruly two year-old does not make you a bad parent.

2. Accept help when it's offered.

3. Your little one has never been two and it can be overwhelming for her. Be patient and look at the person she is becoming rather than the cranky toddler she is today.

4. Always reinforce correction with plenty of hugs and love and say good things about him as well.

Tailor discipline to her personality and design a discipline plan for you, as parents, to consistently implement together.

Toddler Eating and Growing

"In general, my children refuse to eat anything that hasn't danced on television."

- Erma Bombeck

Can you say picky? You may very well find that your toddler is so picky about her food that it confuses even her. At such a crucial time in her development, your baby needs her nutrition more than ever, but sometimes getting her to eat the right things can be a true challenge. This chapter is devoted to remedying that situation with tried and true tips and innovative ideas. So... gobble it all up!

Finicky Foodies

Toddlers are the strangest little beings ever, especially when it comes to food. Most likely, at this stage, your little one is all about food but perhaps only her food of choice. Many a toddler tantrum has resulted over the subject of eating.

Here are ten problems you may encounter.

- Bad table manners (food flying in rage)

- Constipation or diarrhea

- Food allergies

- Gagging

- Power struggles

- Favoring only a select few foods

- Wanting only junk food

- Overweight or underweight

- Excessive pickiness

- Refusal to eat

What can be done? You will find some tips below that can help take a bite out of the problems at hand.

- Be sure she sees you eating a well-rounded diet

- Make meal time fun and stress-free

- Stand your ground, lovingly but firmly

- Make foods fun

- Be creative in the foods you offer her

Toddler Tidbits
Breakfast

Make a pancake and decorate it to ensure your little one's day begins with a smile (and a hearty meal).

Simply add bacon strips to the top for hair, an orange slice for the smile, a berry for the nose and a kiwi for the eyes. There you have the most sunshiny, toddler-friendly breakfast ever!

Breakfast

Cook old-fashion whole grain oatmeal according to the directions on the container. Thin a bit with whole milk. Add a little butter and sweeten with a little brown sugar. Top (or let your toddler top) with
strawberries and blueberries. Yum!

Lunch

Make a splash at lunchtime when you bring out this fun dish.

Simply make her favorite sandwich and cut it in the shape of a fish. Dot the fish eye with a raisin, use shredded carrots for fins and green onion stalks can highlight the tail. Seaweed is made from alfalfa or bean sprouts.

Lunch

Not even a toddler could get angry over this fun lunch. Use a bagel for the base of the bird then add her favorite cold cut and mayo for the white of the eyes and black beans for the eyebrows

and pupils of the eyes. A cheese triangle makes a great nose. There ya go... the perfect happy meal.

Dinner

This octopus is lending a helping hand so you can feed your toddler.

Cut slits on an organic wiener, leaving the top for his head. Dot eyes and a mouth on and let him swim in noodles of any kind. You little one is bound to slurp this fun meal up. Just make sure they take small bites of hot dog!

Dinner

Any main dish will fly when these cute little chicks are served as the side. Simply make deviled eggs and decorate the filling like little chicks. Raisins can be used for eyes and baby carrots for the noses. Lay then on a bed of lettuce and a wonderful dish is hatched.

Snacks

Now we're talking! Cut slices of apples and put two together with peanut butter then add some marshmallow teeth. This is a fun treat near Halloween or any day of the year for that matter.

Snack

It doesn't take much to dress up a healthy snack so that it's irresistible to a curious two year-old. Make adorable little insects like these out of fruit and just add the decorative edible eyes that can be

found in the cake decorating section of many supermarkets. Your little one won't be bugging you anymore. She'll be far too busy munching.

Snack or Dinner

If your little one tends to eat like a bird, you won't have that problem with this fun dish. Simply shape a bird from rice then add carrot slivers for the legs and feet and use a raisin for the eye and a prune peel for the beak. Add crackers and you have a yummy treat your child will peck on until his plate is clean.

Lunch or Dinner

How cool are these hot dogs? All you need to do in order to make them is to shape freezer dinner rolls once they have defrosted and risen. Bake the rolls then add raisins for eyes and nose while still warm. Cut a slit in the middle of the bread and add in a wiener to each on and mustard, if desired.

Festive Snack

Aren't these little guys deliciously adorable? Your child will love them, even if it's not Christmas. They are healthy and easy to make. Banana quarters make the body and raisins make the eyes. The nose can be a dried cranberry or a red candy. Strawberries make the hat and you can use marshmallows for the beard and the bottom and top of the hat (or felt, if you'd rather).

Let's Get Social

Dining with your little one is becoming a social interaction, sometimes good, sometimes not-so-good, but social all the same. Her eating habits should be getting more civil. She can get food to her mouth for the most part and may even be learning some manners. Nutrition continues to be of great importance so make mealtime as enjoyable and fun as possible for the whole family.

Temperamental Twos

Although your child may be a barrel of fun at mealtimes, she may have her moments. It's not unusual for her to suddenly turn from a pea-lover to a pea-hater. She may have detested cottage cheese and now loves it. Her taste buds are changing so find fun ways to introduce new foods and reintroduce ones she has turned down in the past.

How Much and What Should a Two Year-Old Eat?

Although your two year-old's appetite is prone to be sporadic, the rule of thumb is that she needs roughly from 35 to 40 calories per pound of her weight on a daily basis.

Here is exactly what is recommended per day:

- Veggies- 1 cup

- Fruits- 1 cup

- Milk- 2 cups

- Meat and Beans- 2 ounces

Food For Thought

- Food allergies can show up in ways other than skin rashes so be aware of any changes your little one may have when introducing a new food.

- GMO can have negative effects on humans, especially youngsters so going organic is an idea worth considering.

- Little tummies are often gluten-intolerant so if your little one is fretting with digestive issues, talk to her pediatrician and so a little research of your own as well.

- The chart below will give you an idea of the food groups your baby should be eating from and the suggested serving amounts.

... and Growing!

With healthy eating, your baby will be growing and developing so much during the time between 12 and 24 months, it will have you scratching your head. You will wonder how you blinked and she got so big.

Enjoy the time, through trying it may be. It lasts but just a short time. During this year, your child is growing so fast, if you go two weeks without seeing a friend or relative, the next time you see them, they will probably be telling you how much your little one has grown during that short time. And it's true. You won't notice it quite as much because you are with her day in and day out but take a look at pictures taken just a month ago and you will have no doubt. Baby is growing up!

Miraculous Milestones

Below are some things that your baby will most likely be doing this year. If your baby was born premature, it's not unusual to lag behind a little and remember that some little ones excel in some areas and are slower in other areas. Talk to her doctor if you are concerned. Here are some common milestones.

Movement

- Walks by herself with no help

- Runs

- Pulls toys behind her as she walks

- Carries a large toy or several small ones

- Can stand on her tiptoes

- Kicks a ball

- Climbs onto the furniture

- Is able to walk up and down stairs with help

Finger and Hand Skills

- Can hold a crayon or pencil

- Is able to scribble

- Pours out contents of container by turning it upside-down

- Builds tower out of four blocks or more

- Favors one hand

Language

- Can recognize a picture or object

- Recognizes names for familiar objects, body parts and people

- Says some words

- Speaks in 2-4 words sentences (maybe)

- Is able to follow simple commands and instructions

- Is able to use simple phrases

- Repeats words she hears others say

Cognitive

- Can locate easy hidden objects

- Sorts shapes and colors

- Starts to play make-believe

Social and Emotional

- Aware that she is separate from other people

- Imitates the behavior of older children and adults

- Starts to become defiant at times

- Is anxious when separated from you

- Has increasing independence

- Loves to have other children around

Growing Up

Your little one will probably gain about four pounds this year. She will most likely grow about 3-4 inches, too. You will be able to really get an idea of what she will look like, whose eyes she will have and whose body build. Her little personality will be shining through as well. This year is one of the most exciting stages ever so take the time to fully enjoy.

Major and Minor Milestones for Minis

By now, you're probably getting a good idea of if you have a mini version of yourself, your husband or if your little one has physical features all her own that resemble no one in the family. You are most likely getting a good glimpse at other things as well like her little budding personality.

There are some milestones that most babies reach during this year. If your baby hasn't reached them yet or has surpassed them, don't worry. If you are really concerned, mention it to her pediatrician and go from there.

Areas of Progress
Language Skills

From the day she turns one onward, you will notice that she is frequently jabbering nonstop, but only a few words are real words at a time though. But, by the time she is 15-19 months, she should know and understand at least ten times more than she can actually verbalize. Still by the 24 month marker, she'll probably be saying at least 50 words and some 2-words sentences.

Cognitive Abilities

Thinking, learning, reasoning and remembering are all cognitive skills improving throughout the year. She will begin to recall events in the past and recognize symbols and shapes. She will love to mimic  you and others. Her imagination is blossoming and she will engage in pretend.

Physical Growth

It's about the norm that your little one will gain about 3-4 pounds during this year and grow about 3-5 inches as well. Teething will continue. Sorry about that. The molars will be on their way.

Emotional and Social Development

What a cocktail of emotions little ones are. She will experience emotions to the extreme, no matter what they are. If she's happy, she's VERY happy. If she's sad, she's VERY sad. If she's angry, watch out!

She will be much more social. She will delight in being around kids her age, her siblings and grandparents. Sometimes she will be very outgoing and then suddenly be overcome with shyness.

She may also begin to have conflicts in her feelings, especially by the end of the year. She wants to go play but also wants to be with Mommy. She wants to stay up but she wants to take her nap. That is part of the drama of a one year old and if you can, remember that it's not really her fault. That's the wiring of a little one.

Sensory and Motor Development

She will be mastering such things as walking and moving. She will soon be running, hopping and climbing.

More on Feelings and Emotions

Your little one will be dealing with some big emotions. They will confuse her and baffle you much of the time. The chart to the left can help you pinpoint some basic emotions so you can help her get through them. She will need all the help she can get and so will you.

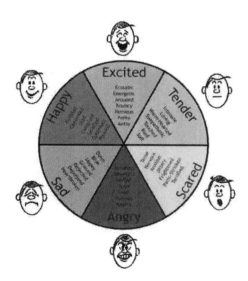

Day Care Bound?

By this age, your child is most likely ready to socialize and learn. He may benefit greatly from play groups as well as preschool type setting day care. At first, you both may struggle a bit with the idea but sometimes it's good to let him experience social and learning settings that are not with you. You may can use a little break anyway. Remember, absence makes the heart grow fonder. He'll be back in your arms in no time.

Your Terrible Two is turning... Terrible Three!

For a year now, you've probably endured the days (and nights) of the terrible twos. "Just five more months," you may have told yourself. Sorry to break it to you, but, if your typical two year-old becomes a typical three year-old, you are most likely in store...for more.

It's all a matter perspective though. As your little one began to gain independence, he ventured out to do such things like telling you "no," throwing tantrums and so forth. Yes indeed, those are unwanted behaviors that require correction. But the root cause is that he is learning and branching out. He is trying out his wings, so to speak.

Here are some dilemmas you may face as your child nears his third birthday:

To nap or not to nap.

Every child's sleeping habits are different. Some require more sleep

than others. As your little one approaches the age of three, he may put up quite a fight when you attempt to put him down for a nap. Even if you put him down for one, sometimes he may still refuse to actually sleep.

The question remains. Should you force your child to nap if he is dead set against it? The answer lies in how he handles *not* napping. Many children will simply fall asleep earlier in the evening when they haven't napped during the day. Others will be holy terrors all the way from what would have been their nap time until bedtime. It's not unusual for a child who hasn't napped to be so out of control by bedtime that he cannot or will not go to sleep at his designated bedtime.

It's a good idea to assess the situation with your child. If he can manage without a nap and his bedtime routine comes around earlier and is fairly smooth sailing, he is probably ready to ditch his nap. But, if you are both miserable when he misses one, by all means, continue to incorporate nap-time as part of his daily schedule, as best you can.

Why?

Especially on a challenging day when you are sleep deprived or stressed out, it will grate on your nerves that your little one sounds like a broken record. "Why?" he asks…about everything. Although to some extent, it is most likely becoming a habit he is getting into, he also genuinely wants to know. By the age of late two and all through the third year, the world is full of wonder for you child… and questions that come along with it. If you do your best to patiently answer the questions, you will be contributing to his first real life lessons. And that... is one of the true joys of parenthood.

Reasoning.

As your baby begins to grow up, you will be able to reason with him more. But, don't expect his reasoning to always line up with your own. He will have his own way of looking at things and from the eyes of a two, almost three year-old, he is always right. There will be times that you can explain things to him and he may even see your point of view, even if he is sure that you are wrong. Other times, however, he will refuse to listen to reason. Choose your battles. To insist that you always "win" will only lead to frustration for both of you. There are, for sure, matters where you will need to stand your ground like when safety is involved. Other times, you may just want to let him be "two... almost three."

Potty Training

Some children are just born ready to be potty trained. Others... not so much. Here are some good signs that your child is ready:

- Is able to stay dry for a few hours at one time

- Shows and interest in the potty

- Is producing more urine at a time than in the past

- Doesn't like to be wet or dirty

- Is able to sit for a few minutes at a time

- Can physically walk

- Signals or tells you he has gone to the potty or needs to go potty

- Shows interest in others going to the restroom

- Wants to wear "big boy" or "big girl" underwear

When you and your child are ready to start his training, it's best to set aside some time to help him along. If you are going on vacation, it's obviously not a great time. But, if you can allot quality time for the endeavor, the chances it will be a success is must greater.

There are tons of tips on potty training techniques. No matter which you choose, your child will need to be asked frequently if she needs to sit on the potty. Both you and she will soon discover about how often but it's a good idea to take her even if she says "no", at least every other time you ask. Asking her will help her feel more involved and somewhat in charge of the process.

When she does go pee or poop in the potty, make a big deal. You and other family members can dish out the praise, applaud, etc. Some children do well by receiving a healthy snack while others like to put a sticker on a potty chart that you can easily make. Still others find the praise and self-gratification to be enough.

Potty training is should certainly be customized to your child. If she is truly ready and some good, quality time is set aside, the process shouldn't take but a week or two. Some of the questions you may come across along the way are:

- If your little boys should sit or stand.

- Whether to use a little potty or the regular toilet.

- If you should put a diaper on him at night.

- Whether you should use pull-up training diapers or not.

- If you should reward him... or not.

These are the questions best answered by you as a mother and... by him as your child. For example, it is quite alright to have your little boy sit... and it is ok to have him stand. It's easier to just sit, providing he gets aimed right but if he can handle the extra duty of standing and aiming, there is nothing wrong with that. There really is no right or wrong answer to any of the questions above.

Of course, there will be accidents. Deal with them as nonchalantly as possible and just keep pushing forward at her own pace. When she gets the hang of it, the two of you will be entering a whole new and wonderful phase... the "no diaper" stage. It will be time for you and your little one to celebrate.

Baby Bump Book

So by now you probably have created and inserted a good bit into your baby's baby book. You've probably got several years in his baby scrapbook completed as well and yes, they are two different books. What? You forgot about his baby book and your scrapbook supplies were taken to the attic when your craft room became a nursery? Well… join the crowd. You are not alone. Don't worry, there will be plenty of time to catch them up… once he goes off to college. Until then, the journey may be a little rough at times, but it's certainly worth every bump along the way.

Chapter Takeaways

1. Milestones are simply to be used as a roundabout measurement. As her social skills emerge, she will be more and more aware that she is a separate individual.

2. This is the age your child will get excited about other little ones being around, beginning to pretend and play with them. She will be a mix of emotions and will feel very strong emotions on a daily basis.

3. Your little one will show signs of readiness when it is time to potty train her. Expect accidents but if you set aside some quality time to help her, all should go very well.

4. Your little one will be mastering the art of walking and getting around. He will develop socially yet will be at conflict as to if he wants to leave your side.

5. Toddlers can be picky eaters, but during the busy toddler stage, your child needs her nutrition more than ever (which may pose a challenge). Be sure to eat a well-rounded diet yourself to set a great example.

One Last Thought

Now that you have read this book, hopefully you feel more prepared for parenthood. You have learned a lot of basics about what having a baby will realistically entail. There will be many sleepless nights, a strain on your marriage and possibly a set or two of grandparents that want to offer unsolicited, unwanted advice.

You have gotten a good look into some not-so-basic aspects about parenting too. You now know that there are a lot of choices you will be faced to make from what type of diaper to use to the method of discipline you'll employ. You now realize that parenthood is a mix of trials and triumphs.

This book may have seemed harsh at times. Although undeniable, your new little miracle will be a joy like none other, it is good to be prepared for the way things will really be, that way, you are able to face everything head on. You should be well on your way to discovering strengths within yourself that will get you through the trying times so you can endure. The rough trails make the mountain top view so much better for we all know that nothing worthwhile is ever truly easy.

Congratulations on reading this book. When you are faced with trials and tribulations of parenthood, you'll now know how to handle them. You won't be caught off-guard and neither will you feel badly because you aren't the perfect parent. You have learned there is no such thing. You are, however, a prepared parent and that is the closest thing there is to a perfect one.